BARRON'S PARENTING KEYS

KEYS TO PARENTING TWINS

Karen Kerkhoff Gromada,
R.N., B.S.N., I.B.C.L.C.

Editor, *Double Talk*

Mary C. Hurlburt

Publisher and Director of Resources
Double Talk Publications

BARRON'S

Cover photo by Scott Barrow, Inc., Cold Spring, NY

DEDICATION

To our husbands, Joe and Barry, and our children who gave us the support and freedom to write this book.

All inquiries should be addressed to:
Barron's Educational Series, Inc.
250 Wireless Boulevard
Hauppauge, New York 11788

Library of Congress Catalog Card No. 91-24413

International Standard Book No. 0-8120-4851-2

Library of Congress Cataloging-in-Publication Data
Gromada, Karen Kerkhoff.
    Keys to parenting twins / Karen Kerkhoff Gromada and Mary C. Hurlburt.
        p. cm. — (Barron's parenting keys)
    Includes index.
    ISBN 0-8120-4851-2
    1. Twins. 2. Child rearing. 3. Infants—Care. 4. Pregnancy.
    I. Hurlburt, Mary C. II. Title. III. Series.

HQ777.35G76 1992   91-24413
649'.144—dc20   CIP

PRINTED IN THE UNITED STATES OF AMERICA
2345   5500   987654321

CONTENTS

INTRODUCTION

Welcome to the exciting world of twin parenting. Twins add a new and very special dimension to the dynamics of a family. Be assured that whatever emotions you feel when you discover you are expecting twins instead of a single child, they are normal! Almost all prospective parents of twins experience both positive and negative feelings. You may be excited one day or hour and petrified the next.

This is a wonderful time to be having twins. You have a better chance of delivering full-term babies with acceptable birth weights than even 10 years ago. The survival rate and normal development for premature, low-birth-weight babies has increased tremendously in the last decade. Not long ago, almost one-third of twin pregnancies went undiagnosed until labor or delivery. With the advent of ultrasound, however, many more twins are diagnosed early in pregnancy. More mothers now receive appropriate prenatal care, and more twins are carried to full term.

Parenting twins is not the same as parenting two children close in age. Your experience is unique. Twins set you apart from other parents. From the beginning parenting twins is more complicated than parenting a single child. Twin pregnancies are monitored more closely. Bonding, or falling in love, with two babies is different from bonding with only one. Getting to know twins includes recognizing and appreciating differences as well as their similarities. This process of differentiation encompasses their looks, personalities, and abilities.

Twins are fascinating. Everyone is intrigued by twins. With the birth of twins, you automatically achieve celebrity status. Friends and strangers alike feel free to make the most pointed comments: "Good grief, double trouble!" They ask the most intimate questions "Were you taking fertility drugs?" They offer the most critical parenting advice: "Can't you control those two?" For the most part you accept all this attention graciously because as parents of twins, you do feel special and you *are*.

Your personal growth is also enormous. Twins are nature's way of teaching organized adults flexibility. You learn to organize and prioritize as you discard the nonessential elements of your life. Twins teach you tolerance and empathy for others who find themselves in unusual situations. You handle new challenges each day, and soon realize you can handle almost anything.

You develop a sense of humor, because you need it. You laugh because your twins do the funniest things. On frantic days, humor may be all that holds you together. As parents of twins you have a different point of reference for raising these children. The issue of their twinship continues to enter into decisions you make regarding either. Twin issues do not disappear as your children mature. Their twinship remains a vital and intimate part of their identities for life. Without appropriate resources, however, parents of twins are left to "reinvent the wheel" as they discover twin-parenting skills.

Our goal in writing this book is to support you, offer practical suggestions, and encourage you to celebrate the individuality of your family and that of each of your twins. We have worked with thousands of parents of twins since our own were born. We have worked through support groups, speaking engagements, and *Double Talk* — a parent-information-sharing international newsletter we began publishing in 1981. This book is a compilation of our personal experiences and the information we have gleaned from these parents. Their experiences and our own have taught us that certain situations frequently arise with the birth of twins, yet each family situation is still unique.

Parenting twins is an experience of a lifetime, and being parents of twins remains part of your identity. Only about 1 in 90 births is a twin birth. You are part of a select group privileged to enjoy this unique "nature versus nurture" parenting experience, addressing the question of whether our genetic makeup or environmental influences have more of an impact on the adults we become. Enjoy it!

Mary C. Hurlburt,
Publisher and Director of Resources
Double Talk Publications

Karen Kerkhoff Gromada, R.N., B.S.N., I.B.C.L.C.
Editor, *Double Talk*

1

~~~~~~

TWIN DEVELOPMENT

The diagnosis is definite. There are two babies growing inside you. How did this happen? What leads to the conception of twins? How did you come to be the lucky one? This Key discusses how twins develop and who is more likely to conceive them.

Conception

Identical twins. Science does not know why identical twinning occurs, but it does know how it occurs. Identical twins begin life the same as a single infant. One sperm cell fertilizes one egg (ovum) cell. Fertilization results in a new single cell called the zygote, which begins to rapidly divide—first into two cells, then four, eight, sixteen, and so on. At some point in the process of early cell division, half of the zygotic cells separate completely from the other half. Now there are two zygotes instead of one.

For approximately 25% of identical twins, the single zygote separates into two while still in a fallopian tube. These identical twin zygotes then implant separately in the uterine lining. Because of this, each has a separate placenta and a separate amniotic sac that is composed of a separate amnion layer and chorion layer.

The big split takes place after uterine implantation of the still single zygote for almost 75% of identical twins. This is the reason most identical twins share one placenta and the chorionic layer of the amniotic sac, but each is within a separate amnion layer of the sac. Only 1 to 2% of identical twins share an amnion as well as a chorion.

1

Another name for identical twins is *monozygotic* twins, which means "one-zygote twins." Because each monozygotic twin develops from the original fertilized egg, 100% of their genetic material is the same. This is why identical twins are always the same sex, look alike, and have similar temperaments. It is usually difficult to tell identical twins apart until you know each one well.

Fraternal twins. Fraternal twins result when two separate eggs (ova) released at ovulation are fertilized by two different sperm in the fallopian tube(s). These two different zygotes travel to and implant separately in the uterine lining. Each always develops a separate placenta, amnion, and chorion. Sometimes the two zygotes implant next to one another and their placentas fuse, so they may appear to share a single placenta when there are actually two placentas.

Another name for fraternal twins is dizygotic twins, which means "two-zygote twins." *Dizygotic twins* are essentially full siblings who happen to inhabit the uterus at the same time and share the same birthday. These twins share approximately 50% of the same genetic material. This is the same number of genes that any full siblings share. *Fraternal twins* can be the same or different sexes, and they may look as much alike or unalike as any brothers and sisters.

Who has twins?

The incidence of monozygotic twinning is about the same for women of every ethnic group and culture. Neither heredity nor any other factor seems to influence its occurrence. There are reports of several sets of identical twins, however, within some extended families, a phenomenon unlikely to occur by chance alone.

Many factors influence dizygotic twinning rates. All are related to the releasing of more than one mature egg at ovulation. You are more likely to produce two eggs and conceive dizygotic twins if you: (1) have a family history of fraternal twins on your mother's side; (2) have already given birth to dizygotic twins; (3) conceive after 35 years of age; (4) have had several other pregnancies; (5) conceive within the first three months of marriage; and/or (6) conceive during your first spontaneous menstrual cycle after discontinuing birth control pills. Black women have a higher dizygotic twinning rate than whites, and whites have a higher rate than Asians.

Women taking *ovulatory induction agents*, so-called fertility drugs, have a significantly higher rate of dizygotic twinning. These medications promote the maturation of more than one egg per menstrual cycle. Fertility may be enhanced by taking one of these medications alone, or the medication may be combined with a surgical technique, such as in vitro fertilization (IVF), gamete intrafallopian transfer (GIFT), or embryo transfer (ET). It also is possible for a single zygote, conceived after its mother took an ovulatory induction agent, to split and form identical twins.

While the monozygotic twinning rate remains about 1 per 250 live births, the dizygotic twinning rate has increased slightly in the last 10 to 20 years. Twenty years ago 1.4% of the live births in this country were twins. Now 2.4% are twins. This 1% jump reflects a rise in fraternal twin births. It is thought to be related to a greater number of women postponing childbearing until their thirties and advances in infertility treatment.

Determining twin type

Many parents are not certain whether they have identical or fraternal twins, so the statistics are not completely accurate. (For more information on determining twin type, see Key 22.)

3

2

BEGIN TO THINK
OF TWO

Your body may tell you to start thinking in terms of two babies long before your twins are born. The normal changes of pregnancy are often exaggerated with your twin pregnancy. Abdominal dimensions double to accommodate two, so expect to look like you are carrying twins! Your size reinforces that you deserve extra consideration.

Body changes

Women seldom breeze through a twin pregnancy, experiencing no more discomfort than a woman carrying a single child. Increased pregnancy hormone levels affect more than your uterus alone. You may experience more of the symptoms of pregnancy and experience them to a greater degree. Expect to have some of the following: nausea in early pregnancy, constipation, backache, headaches, heartburn, swelling of extremities, pelvic pressure, and/or a bruised feeling through your pelvic area during the last month. Discuss these symptoms with your obstetrician or midwife if you have any concerns.

Eating for three

You are eating for three so it is important to significantly increase your caloric intake. An improved diet during pregnancy helps your body return to its pre-pregnancy weight. Eat tuna and egg salad instead of processed meat; fruit instead of candy; fresh vegetables instead of potato chips.

Drink juice and water instead of coffee or soda. Broil and bake instead of frying. One mother who gained 40 pounds during the last four months of her pregnancy was admonished by her doctor to watch her weight. "But I knew," she said, "that my diet was better than it had ever been. Within a week of my twins' birth, I lost that 40 pounds plus another 10 without even trying!" (See Key 5.)

Early bonding

Early diagnosis of your twin pregnancy helps you prepare both mentally and physically for the birth of two individual babies. To enhance early bonding, ask for a photograph or video recording of your ultrasound scan. Leave the photo where you can look at it often. Take your husband to your ultrasound appointment and watch the video with him. Thinking about two babies helps you both adjust to the idea before they get here.

Get to know your babies before they arrive. Take time to notice the movement and placement of each one in your uterus. Watch them move. Share the experience with your twins' father. This makes twins seem real to him too.

Read all that you can about twins before your twins arrive. When you are better informed about twin pregnancy and delivery and raising twins, you can create a better situation for their homecoming. Start now to think of names and what your approach to raising twins will be. Discuss your excitement and any anxieties with your spouse.

Classes

Take an early pregnancy class to gain a better understanding of your current body changes and what to expect during the rest of pregnancy. Tell your instructor that you are expecting twins so she can address your unique situation.

Attend "prepared" childbirth classes earlier than is usually suggested. Premature delivery is not unusual with twins, so be prepared. If your instructor knows you are expecting twins, she should have some special guidelines for you. Take a special class for cesarean delivery as well. Be prepared for all possible birth experiences. There now are more cesarean than vaginal twin deliveries. (See Keys 4 and 10.)

If you plan to breastfeed, you need information for getting off to the best start. Take a special class if available, and contact a local La Leche League leader or a certified lactation consultant. Do not let others discourage you with remarks like, "You won't have enough milk for two babies." (See Key 14.)

If handling babies is a new experience for you, contact your local Red Cross. They teach basic infant care classes. You and your spouse will feel more at ease with your babies if you know how to handle them when they arrive home.

Plan ahead

Arrange for full-time household help for the first week or two after you bring your twins home from the hospital. Your husband can take vacation time, one of the grandmothers may want to come, or you may need to hire help. You *will* need someone with you!

Most mothers of twins report that if they had anything to do over again, they would continue to have household help well beyond the early postpartum period, even if they had to borrow money to hire someone. Accepting help is difficult for some women, especially if they are not employed outside the home. If you resist the idea or cannot afford a cleaning service, consider hiring a high school student or a senior citizen for routine help. Ask them to help with the housekeeping, not caring for the babies. You need to save that for yourself.

Make meals now and freeze them so you can pop them into the microwave or oven after your twins' arrival. If friends offer to bring in meals say, "Yes!" They can leave meals in nonreturnable containers before or after the babies' birth. One friend could coordinate the effort so someone different fixes a meal each night after the babies arrive home. Take advantage of all offers of help.

Contact a local Mothers of Twins Club. There is nothing like talking with someone who has been there. (See Appendix B: Resources.)

You cannot prepare for all possible situations. No experience compares with this one, but flexibility, knowledge, and preparation are the keys to a smoother transition to life with two infants.

3

PARENT AND DOCTOR TEAMWORK

You and your physician or nurse midwife are an inseparable team when it comes to developing strategies for the safest possible pregnancy and birth for you and your babies. You both play equally important and complementary roles. The physician and nurse midwife contribute professional expertise, and you know your body better than they. Also, these are your babies and you will be responsible for their care during the next twenty plus years.

Pregnancy and childbirth are major life events intimately entwined with female sexuality. The impact of these experiences lasts a lifetime. It is only right that you, the person most affected by these events, should decide on the degree of your involvement in any decision making during this time. Your husband should voice his thoughts as well. His stake in this pregnancy is as great as yours.

Self-care participation

How can you participate in your medical care if you have no medical background? There are several things anyone can do: (1) examine your personal needs and goals for this experience; (2) read everything you can about twin pregnancy and childbirth; and (3) ask health care providers every possible question related to the experience.

Personal needs and goals. Consider your answers to these or similar questions. How much do you want to be involved in, or in control of, your experience? What are your personal goals for this pregnancy and birth, and how can you meet them? Take this question beyond the normal desire for healthy babies.

Once you have a better idea of your goals, question your health care provider. Does your obstetrician have a routine or a flexible approach to multiple pregnancies? What is your physician's rate of vaginal versus cesarean twin births? Do your delivery and anesthesia options change because you are having twins? If yes, how do they change? What differences might you expect or need to consider that parents having a single baby would not? How can you best prepare for the various situations related to a twin childbirth?

What options are available at the hospital where you will deliver? Which options will help you meet your goals? Ask if the hospital is well equipped for all idiosyncrasies associated with twin births. For example, does this hospital's newborn intensive care nursery (NICU) keep all premature and sick newborns, or are some transferred? How far away is the best-equipped NICU? Does your doctor have delivery privileges there? Would you and your babies be safer in a hospital prepared for all complications? How do you feel about the possibility of separation from your babies if one or both are transferred to an outside NICU?

Develop birth plans for several possible situations. Plans should cover the full-term, vaginal birth of both; premature labor; emergency cesarean of one or both; one or both sick newborns; and maternal complications. Make a copy of the plans you and your doctor agree upon for your husband, the doctor (and any medical partners), and your hospital labor chart.

9

Reading material. Several books for parents of twins are now available. A couple of these focus on twin pregnancy and childbirth. Most medical texts contain a few helpful tidbits; but, these tend to focus on detecting and treating rather than preventing the complications more commonly associated with twin pregnancies. For more information, refer to Appendix A: Suggested Reading and Keys 4 and 5.

Questions. You cannot ask your doctor or midwife too many questions. Besides asking general questions related to your needs and goals, question *all* treatment recommendations. Ask open-ended questions that begin with "who," "what," "where," "when," "how," and "why," because these require detailed explanations.

Ask, "Why do you recommend I. . .gain *X* pounds; eat this diet; have serial ultrasounds; quit work early; initiate bed rest; take medication to prevent or halt premature labor; be examined vaginally every week; monitor uterine contractions; count fetal movements periodically; or go for weekly nonstress tests?"

Why ask "Why"? Many of the treatments typically recommended during a twin pregnancy are controversial. Research results related to such issues as ideal maternal weight gain, the use of medications to prevent (not halt) premature labor, or the initiation of bed rest are inconclusive. Different doctors define certain terms or treatments differently. Also, it is your prerogative to get a second opinion or change professionals if you are ever uncomfortable with a doctor's advice or approach.

You are not bothering your doctor or midwife when you ask questions. This is your body, your babies. Any doctor who feels secure in his or her knowledge and abilities welcomes questions. This physician recognizes that not only do you have a right and a responsibility to care for yourself and your unborn babies, you are also more likely to comply with a treatment regimen when you understand the reasons behind it.

Other concerns

Let your physician know how you feel about having twins. Do not keep to yourself any fears regarding the eventual outcome of the pregnancy or taking two babies home. Look to your physician as a resource for: additional written information, contacting organizations of twin parents and other parenting groups, or locating professional counseling services.

The final analysis

Not everyone wants the same thing from twin pregnancy and childbirth. You may demand an active decision-making role or prefer to take a backseat. No one can tell you how to feel or how involved to be. However, it is vitally important that you, as parents, and your medical professional feel comfortable within this relationship. If you are satisfied with the way your physician handles routine questions and situations, you will have more trust in the doctor's judgment if an unexpected situation arises.

It takes teamwork to achieve the healthiest outcome for you and your twins. Neither you nor your doctor can do it alone. Your physician or midwife needs your input to tailor medical and nursing care to you and your babies' needs. A physician's expertise is only as good as your willingness to follow a recommended treatment plan. Expect to receive the best medical care for your unique situation only if you take the time to analyze your feelings and understand any medical recommendations.

4

RISK FACTORS

Many obstetricians automatically label twin pregnancies as "high risk." Being placed in this category means only that the potential for development of several pregnancy and birth complications is higher than for a woman having a single baby. It does not mean that you or your babies definitely will experience complications.

Common complications

The most common complications for infants associated with twin pregnancy are preterm (premature) labor and birth and intrauterine growth retardation (IUGR). Pregnancy-induced hypertension, often referred to as preeclampsia or toxemia of pregnancy, affects more women experiencing a twin pregnancy. Let's look at each of these problems separately. (See Key 5.)

Preterm labor. A normal pregnancy lasts 38 to 42 weeks. This also is called the *gestation period.* A baby born before 37 weeks' gestation is considered preterm. Preterm delivery is associated with immaturity of infant physical systems and low birth weight. According to the most recent statistics from the National Center for Health Statistics, in 1988 45% of twins versus 9.4% of single-born infants were delivered before 37 weeks. The average length of gestation was 36.2 weeks for twins as opposed to 39.3 weeks for one infant.

Intrauterine growth retardation. An infant weighing less than normal for the week of gestation is considered growth retarded. Statistically, twins and single infants follow the same growth curve until 30 to 35 weeks of gestation, at which time the growth rates begin to decline. Twins generally weigh less or are "small for gestational age" (SGA) compared to single infants, even when they are born after 37 weeks. Often one twin is affected more than the other. This is particularly true for identical (monozygotic) twins sharing a single placenta. Connections between blood vessels in their placenta can result in a disproportionate amount of oxygen and nutrients reaching one twin, which is called *twin transfusion syndrome.* The effect of these vessel-to-vessel connections varies depending on the type of blood vessels involved and the degree to which it occurs. Even when there are two placentas, one placenta may provide greater access to oxygen and nutrients for one twin. This usually results in different growth rates for each twin.

Pregnancy-induced hypertension (PIH). PIH is two-to-three times more likely to develop during twin pregnancies than single ones. The cause of this condition is not understood, but it is characterized by several physical changes in the expectant mother. These include a sharp increase in the mother's blood pressure, protein in her urine, and a sudden, large weight gain related to fluid retention.

Implications. All of these complications are associated with an increased incidence of low-birth-weight twins, which is defined as a birth weight of 5 pounds, 8 ounces (2500 grams) or less. (Some experts believe this should be raised to six pounds or less.) In 1988 50.2% of twins compared to 6% of single infants were considered low birth weight. Low birth weight is of concern because affected infants are more likely to experience physical, emotional, and cognitive developmental delays.

The risks realistically

Many expectant mothers have very healthy, uncomplicated twin pregnancies. Concentrate on the fact that 55% of twins are born at or after 37 weeks of pregnancy and that almost half weigh more than 5 pounds, 8 ounces (2500 grams). Realize that after hearing for months that you can expect to deliver early, it may be as much of a shock to find yourself among those 13.6% who deliver at 40 or more weeks of gestation and/or the almost 20% having one or both twins weighing over 6 pounds, 11 ounces (3000 grams). Incidentally, if you are among this group, it does no good to poke at your abdomen while telling your unborn babies, "Hey, you can come out now!"

5

DECREASING THE RISKS

Twin pregnancy risk factors automatically decrease if you enter the pregnancy as a well-nourished nonsmoker enjoying good general health. Your prepregnancy health is related to a well-functioning cardiovascular system. This system in turn is essential for the development and maintenance of one large or two single placentas that supply your twins with oxygen and nutrients from your circulation. Healthy placentas and a healthy twin pregnancy go together.

The physical changes of pregnancy that support placental function increase during twin pregnancy. A greater amount of fluid circulates through your blood vessels (expanded blood volume), a larger uterine area is covered by the placenta(s), and nutritional reserves are increased. Your diet affects each of these changes. Many experts believe diet plays a crucial role in helping placentas remain healthy so that twin pregnancies have a better chance to reach full term.

What you can do

You are not getting fat; you are growing two babies! You need lots of calories and extra protein to do this properly—about 3000 to 4000 calories and over 100 grams of protein daily. Eat enough for the three of you.

Your weight gain is one indicator of how well your body is adapting to your twin pregnancy. Among mothers surveyed for a recent study, those who delivered twins at term gained an average of 47 to 49 pounds; but their infants' birth weights were not reported. A 50 to 60 pound gain is common for those delivering normal-weight full-term twins.

If you were underweight when you conceived, you may need to gain additional weight. Twin pregnancies for women of average or slightly above average weight or height are more likely to reach full term.

You may gain a steady amount each month, or you might alternate smaller and larger gains at various points during your twin pregnancy. Your weight gain pattern is uniquely your own. Do not worry about larger weight gains as long as your blood pressure stays within normal limits, you have no sudden body swelling, and your tested urine is fine.

Do not diet to limit your weight gain. Eat foods in as close to their natural state as possible to avoid empty calories, unnecessary additives, and hidden salt. You will not have to worry about postpartum weight loss if you eat "good" foods now.

You may feel full quickly if your twins press on your stomach. If so, eat several small meals rather than three large meals each day.

You can monitor your fluid intake by checking the color of your urine: pale yellow indicates a good fluid intake; dark yellow urine means you need more fluid.

Just as twin pregnancy changes are exaggerated, anything you put into your mouth can have an exaggerated *positive* or *negative* effect on the health and function of your placenta. This includes nonfood items, such as vitamins, tobacco, caffeine, alcohol and all medications, whether prescription, over-the-counter, or "street" drugs.

See Appendix A: Suggested Reading for books emphasizing diet information for twin pregnancy.

What you need to know—just in case

Even if you do everything right, sometimes complications still occur. Most medical treatments or tests focus on the early detection of such complications. You can be involved by becoming aware of the signs that signal potential problems.

Preterm labor. Premature delivery of twins can sometimes be postponed or avoided if you know its signs. Do not wait to see if preterm labor stops. Call your medical professional *immediately* if you experience even *one* of these signs:

- intermittent or continuous pelvic pressure;
- any increased vaginal discharge;
- low backache or cramping; and/or
- four or more uterine contractions (tightening or "balling up" of the uterus) within an hour.

Twin growth and development. You can help your doctor keep an eye on your twins' development by counting both babies' movements. Become sensitive to each twin's position within your uterus, and then count each one's movements during a specified time period every day beginning at 28 weeks' gestation:

- Count each twin's movements until each moves 10 times.
- Chart how long it takes for each to move 10 times.

If one or both does not move 10 times within two hours or either takes progressively longer to move 10 times, *immediately* notify your obstetrician or nurse midwife. This does not mean there is a definite problem, but it does indicate an immediate need for further testing.

Maternal pregnancy-induced hypertension. For the early detection of pregnancy-induced hypertension (PIH), keep all prenatal medical appointments so your blood pressure and urine can be monitored. Report immediately any sudden swelling of your body, abdominal pain in the area of your rib cage, severe headaches, seeing spots, or loss of eyesight.

Controversial interventions. Routinely advising bed rest to prevent complications during twin pregnancy is very controversial, as the research results on this topic are contradictory. Some experts believe bed rest takes weight off the cervix and increases blood flow to the placentas. Others say it interferes with placental function, since women on bed rest tend to eat fewer calories and drink less.

In recent years, some physicians have begun to recommend two other highly controversial treatments in an effort to prevent preterm twin labor. These include *routinely:* (1) prescribing tocolytic drugs—medications that stop or slow preterm labor once it occurs, or (2) inserting a stitch called a cerclage to hold the cervix closed. No research supports the use of either of these treatments as a method to *prevent* preterm labor with twin pregnancies.

Any of these controversial treatments may be prescribed appropriately under certain conditions to prevent preterm delivery. Always discuss their use in depth with your doctor. (See Key 3.)

You make a difference

You can decrease the possibility of complications by becoming well informed and involved in your own prenatal care. You do not have to "wait and see" what happens. You can make a healthy difference. (See Key 4.)

6

~~~~~~

CHOOSING PEDIATRIC CARE

Shop for a supportive pediatrician, family physician, or pediatric nurse practitioner before your twins' expected arrival. You and your twins will spend lots of time and money at a medical professional's office in the next few years, so you need to find someone with whom you feel comfortable and confident. Choosing a medical professional with a reassuring personality and a compatible child care philosophy is as important as ensuring that your twins' doctor has the appropriate medical credentials. This Key will give you ideas for finding someone well suited to both you and your twins' needs.

Your obstetrician, friends with children, and members of the local Mothers of Twins Club or La Leche League group are good starting points for pediatric care recommendations. You also want to consider the convenience of a physician's office location. Keep in mind, however, that it is not a good idea to choose your twins' doctor based *only* on the convenient location of the doctor's office or another's recommendation.

Begin to interview pediatricians or family physicians during the middle months of your twin pregnancy, because of the greater possibility of preterm delivery. Many physicians encourage a prenatal parent visit, some may prefer to talk with expectant parents over the telephone, and others ask one of their personnel to handle these interviews. A physician's attitude about meeting or talking with you before your babies' birth tells you a great deal about a doctor's approach.

Ask if the practice includes a certified pediatric nurse practitioner (CPNP) and consider interviewing her for your twins' well-baby care. This service is generally less expensive than a physician's, and a CPNP often has more time to discuss your questions and concerns.

You have more medical professional options if you live in an urban area. This does not mean that you should not interview the only physician available in a small rural town. You still learn a lot by talking with the physician who will care for your babies before they actually arrive.

You might want to know if a particular medical practice has cared for many sets of twins. Ask physicians whether they have found any child care issues to be of particular concern for parents of twins. This gives you an idea of a doctor's sensitivity to your unique situation.

Ask if the medical practice offers a discount on fees for twins. Many doctors recognize the financial strain that two well-baby visits place on a family. These physicians charge the full amount for each baby's immunizations and for the first twin's physical examination, but they deduct 50 to 100% from the second twin's exam. Other medical practices charge the full amount for both visits.

If you are breastfeeding, you will feel more confident if your babies' medical professionals have a positive attitude about breastfeeding twins. How many twins in the practice have been breastfed? What does the physician or CPNP think about breastfeeding twins? What attitude does the doctor or nurse have about complementary or supplementary formula or starting two on solid foods? Does the practice employ or recommend a certified lactation consultant (CLC)? Does the practice recommend contacting a breastfeeding support group, such as La Leche League?

Visit the pediatrician's office. Check its physical arrangements. How easy would it be to take two infants from the car to the office without another adult accompanying you? Are there ramps and elevators that can accommodate a twin stroller, or must you use stairs at some point? How many doors must you go through, and are they easy to open?

Ask if the pediatric office has a separate waiting area for children suspected of having contagious diseases. Since you end up caring for two sick babies if either twin brings a communicable disease home from the doctor's, you have more reason to avoid unnecessary illnesses!

Because you will be keeping track of two children in the waiting room, ask the receptionist which appointment time is best to request so your twins can be seen more quickly. Usually the first appointments in the morning and after the lunch break are seen immediately. After those appointments the waiting area may back up.

Is there a special time during the day or week when you can call to ask general questions regarding your twins' growth or care? While sorting through the unique idiosyncrasies of two new individuals, you are bound to have more questions and concerns than the parents of a single infant. Some medical practices set aside a special hour or two to help with these nonemergency issues. This way parents do not have to worry that they are "bothering" the doctor.

No one physician is best for all babies or parents. If you are ever unhappy with your twins' medical care for whatever reason, it is your prerogative to take them to another pediatric practice. By taking the time before the twins' birth to interview physicians, you are more likely to be satisfied.

7

NAMING YOUR TWINS

Naming twins, as with every other aspect of raising twins, is more complicated than naming a single child. If you know before their births that there are two, then you have all kinds of name combinations to think of. Mothers often tell stories similar to this one:

> The attendants in the delivery room laughed when my first son was born and I said, "Wait until the next one comes and I'll tell you if his name is Thomas or Michael." If his twin had been a girl, Michael would have been been named Thomas, Jr. instead of Michael.

Carefully consider the names you give your babies. Don't choose the second twin's name merely to balance the first. A name separates us from the masses and identifies us as unique individuals. A twin's name also sets him apart from that other person who is often regarded as his other half. We all want to know that our name was chosen especially for us and that it has some significance to our parents.

Initially, it may sound like fun to name your babies something "twinny"—Ronnie and Donnie (rhyming), Rose and Violet (both flowers), Steve and Stephanie (male and female versions of the same name), John Adam and Jennifer Amelia (same initials), Alex and Andy (assonance) or Jennifer and Jessica (alliteration). Twin names may encourage people to view twins as a unit instead of two individuals. Is your goal to raise two individuals who are proud of their twinship, but not limited to it, or to reinforce the unit?

Parents who discover "It's twins!" in the delivery room are particularly prone to giving their babies rhyming names. One adult twin said she was named Kammy because her parents had already chosen the name Tammy for a girl. When another daughter popped out, the father just announced, "Well, I guess she's Kammy then!" This is natural and certainly forgivable. After all, it's quite a surprise to discover you have two babies instead of one.

Interviews with adult twins indicate that although some resent twinny names, others do not mind in the least. If your babies are not here yet, consider these factors when making your choices.

- Twinny names—Mary and Barry—discourage individuality. They also lead to confusion since they sound so much alike. Just imagine the number of times in a lifetime you may hear, "Who?" or "I thought you wanted him, not me!"
- Friends, relatives, and teachers have difficulty remembering which name goes with which twin, especially if the names rhyme or have the same cadence. This happens even with fraternal twins. One teacher said that it took her months to remember which twin was Mandy and which was Wendy even though the girls barely looked like sisters.
- Giving boy/girl twins the male/female version of the same name—Steve and Stephanie—also encourages others to view the twins as a unit.
- In this age of computers, having the same initials as one's twin confuses record keeping. A pharmacist had to change the birth date of one twin in his computer because the family insurance carrier kept refusing reimbursement for identical prescriptions, claiming duplicate forms were sent.
- If you are a father who desperately wants a junior and has twin sons, consider the impact for the twin not named for his father. This can become a very intense point when

choosing names. One father was so desperate for a junior that when he realized his baptismal certificate listed his full name, Benjamin Francis, and his birth certificate listed the shortened, Ben Frank, he wanted to name each a junior. (He finally settled on not having a junior.)

- Cute baby "nicknames" may stay with children for a lifetime and may not be appreciated in adulthood.
- Give your twins currently popular names, and you may be adding another element to their identity problems. By the time twins Christopher and Jason entered first grade, their parents knew they had chosen the area's two most popular names. In their class of 16 boys there were four Jasons and three Christophers. The boys' best friends were also named Jason and Christopher. Even going to the pool or park was a comedy. Calling for "Chris" or "Jason" produced the turning of a dozen little heads.
- Be aware of other classifications of names as well. It may be better to stick to two ethnic names (Omer and Katarina), trendy names (Tiffany and Lindsay), unisex names (Baily and Casey), and gender-specific names (Joseph and Catherine) for both.
- Naming your twins after special people in your lives, such as grandparents, is a nice idea if you like both names. This isn't the time to exclude one, however. The twin not named for a loved one will wonder why, and the grandparent left out may feel offended.
- Finally, while making your decision, say the two names aloud. Do they sound right together? Do the names flow easily no matter which is said first? The same child does not want to be second in rotation every time.

Remember that many people grow up with names they do not appreciate. You want your twins to know that a lot of thought went into your choices. This relieves you of guilt if either hates his name at some period in his life.

8

~~~~~~

BABY CARE PRODUCTS

I f the thought of buying two of everything panics you, relax. Having twins is more expensive than having one child, but it is not prudent or necessary to buy everything new or to double all your purchases. Most Mothers of Twins Clubs sponsor semiannual sales of well-maintained infant clothing and equipment. Garage sales and church bazaars are also good sources. The following is a list of essential and helpful items.

Layette

The twins' layette does not have to be elaborate. About 10 stretch sleepers or cotton gowns and an equal number of T-shirts is enough for most newborn twins. You probably need several receiving blankets and one crib blanket for each baby. Several crib sheets are a must. Each baby needs a sweater and a hat, and a snowsuit if it is cold.

Diapers

Two babies use twice as many diapers as a single baby. Each newborn needs to be changed approximately 100 times per week. If you use disposable diapers, the cost is doubled, but they are convenient and available in sizes from premie through toddler.

You do not need to buy twice as many diapers if you wash your own. You simply must wash them twice as often. Washing diapers soon becomes part of your daily routine.

The more diapers you use, the more economical diaper service becomes. The initial delivery charge does not change because you have two babies. The cost of additional diapers is usually minimal. Check with the services in your area. You may discover that a diaper service is the least expensive option when you have twins.

Car seats

Two car seats meeting federal guidelines for safety are a *must*. You save money if you purchase seats that serve your babies from birth through the toddler years. Consider your car when you choose a particular model. Some do not work with certain seat belts, and others are so big that two do not fit in the car.

Cribs

Your twins can share a crib during their early months and maybe even later. Some twins sleep better when allowed to cuddle. Between three and six months they may begin to disturb each other. Any crib purchased or borrowed should meet government guidelines for safety. Slats must be no more than 2⅜ inches apart because babies can strangle themselves if their heads slip through the slats (your twins' heads may be small as a result of prematurity or low birth weight). Also, cribs should be free of projections that may catch on infants' clothing.

Stroller

Invest in a good twin stroller. Twins use a stroller longer and more often because no parent has enough eyes or hands to manage two unconfined infants, toddlers, or preschoolers. The following is a list of the different types of strollers, with their advantages and disadvantages.

Some limousine-type strollers are heavy and long. Most are easy to push but require effort to get one in and out of a car. Either your twins face each other or both face forward.

Both seats fully recline. Most are comfortable even for newborns, but some brands provide little leg room for toddler twins.

You can maneuver a side-by-side stroller that is less than 36 inches wide through most doorways and aisles. Many come with seats that fully recline so babies are safe and comfortable from birth. Some models weigh less than 20 pounds, collapse easily, and take up little space in your car.

Some double strollers are designed for use by a toddler and an infant. Both seats usually face forward and only one seat fully reclines. These work nicely once both babies are able to sit up and they are often less expensive than true twin strollers. Meanwhile, one baby can be in an infant carrier while the other rides in the stroller. (See Key 33.)

When you search for a double stroller, ask friends to recommend brand names. If you cannot find a twin style of a preferred brand, go to a specialty shop carrying that brand. They should be willing to special order a twin stroller from the manufacturer. Check their return policy on specially ordered items before placing the order. You may be forced to keep a stroller you do not want.

Infant carrier

There are some specially designed infant twin carriers. The most practical zip apart so they can be used as either a single or a twin carrier. (See Keys 31 and 33.)

Other equipment

- Changing tables are nice, but they are not essential to perform the task. A clean towel, piece of flannel sheeting, or a changing pad on the floor, sofa, or bed will do just as well.
- An infant swing may keep one twin pleasantly occupied while you feed the other. If you have two swings you may

be able to sneak some time for your own meals. *However, never leave your babies unattended in swings!*

- Infant seats, especially those that bounce, are helpful. You can bottlefeed your babies while they rest in infant seats. You can hold one baby and breast or bottlefeed, while gently bouncing the other with your foot.

- A single playpen is generally too small to confine two active babies, but placing your newborns in a playpen protects them from older siblings. Later, they are great for storing toys or keeping one twin confined while tending to the other.

Nonessential equipment

Walkers, jumpers, bouncers, and other items are nonessential equipment. Walkers especially are associated with a high incidence of accidents and visits to emergency rooms.

Buy only the essentials before your babies are born. Accept friends' equipment on loan. After the twins are here, you have a better idea what equipment works for you and your babies.

9

RETURNING TO WORK

Many mothers return to the work force shortly after the birth of a baby. Whether you plan to return to work out of economic necessity, an emotional need to be employed, or to save your place on the corporate ladder, the birth of twins adds another dimension to your decision and your arrangements. Child care arrangements should be made while you are pregnant. You probably will be too busy and too tired after their births.

A twin pregnancy and childbirth is more stressful for your body than a pregnancy and childbirth for a single baby. You will probably sleep less than the mother of a single baby. Your time with each baby is divided when you are relating to two. Returning to work divides your time and energy even more. Spending a lot of time with your babies during the early months is essential if you are to get to know your two individual babies, so build babies' time into your employment plans. (See Keys 23 and 24 for more information.)

Review your options

While you make employment plans, consider options that minimize child care costs and expenses. You may find it helpful to ask yourself the following questions.

- After deducting child care costs and other job-related expenses, how much disposable income do you have? The birth of twins may mean that it costs almost as much for both parents to work as it does for one to stay home, at least until they are toddlers. Child care for infant twins is generally very expensive. When you add up the cost of child care, a working wardrobe, transportation to and from work, and meals out, staying home may cost less than you think.

- You may want to consider postponing your return to work. Can you extend your maternity leave? Would taking an unpaid leave of absence be a good option for you?
- Can you arrange your work schedules so that one or the other parent is home with the babies for most of the day? Can either of you switch to an afternoon shift? Would your employer agree to a flextime arrangement? If you think a specific arrangement will work better for you, it does not hurt to ask.
- Can you introduce the concept of job sharing, with you and another coworker each working part time at the same job? Although it may not be your company's policy now, some companies are willing to be flexible because job sharing between two trained employees is cheaper than training someone new.
- Would working part time instead of full time for a time benefit you and your babies? This arrangement gives you extra time to spend with the babies, your body has more time to recover, and you remain visible in the work force. Perhaps you can arrange to work part-time hours while your spouse is home with the babies.
- Do you have a job skill that enables you to make money working from home? You need a mother's helper to enforce your work time, but this way you are there for emergencies and to offer a helping hand when needed, while still being gainfully employed.

Considerations

If Grandma or Grandpa wants to watch your twins, you have the ideal situation. They will be cared for by an experienced parent, who adores them just as you do. Unfortunately, in today's world, this is not usually an option. Consider the following when you think about day care.

- Ultimately, you are responsible for your children even if you relinquish their care to someone else for part of the day. Clearly state your expectations with regard to raising twins and developing individuality to the sitter.

- Consider live-in child care help if you work full time. This is no longer reserved for the rich especially when you calculate the cost of day care for two children. Many families have had successful experiences with an au pair.

- You need someone who adores babies and will interact with each infant twin. If this person comes to your home, do not expect her to perform light housekeeping as well. She probably will not have the time.

- If your babies are going to a day-care provider, consider finding one close to the work place instead of close to home. You gain time to interact with your babies during travel, and occasionally you may be able to visit them for a feeding. This is especially helpful for the breastfeeding mother. (See Keys 13 and 14.)

- Are you able to make special arrangements for day care if the babies are sick? Studies show that children in day care are often ill more than children who remain in their own homes. Many parents use their own sick days when children are ill, but between them, your twins may be sick so often that you will not have enough sick days.

- Interview several care givers. Some providers give a break for the second twin. This is not where you want to scrimp. You are placing precious possessions in the sitter's care.

10

~~~~~~

D (ELIVERY) DAY
AT LAST

The big day is here. Today is your twins' birthday whether Mother Nature alone decides the date or she is given a nudge by you and your doctor. If you are like most of us, you have been looking forward to this day with both incredible excitement and some trepidation. This Key gives you some idea of what to expect.

Admission

Your doctor already sent information about your pregnancy to the labor and delivery unit, so they know to prepare for two babies. Bring a copy of your birth plan to place on your chart. Go over the details of the plan with the nurse who will follow you during labor and delivery. (See Key 3.)

The hospital staff prepares for all delivery possibilities. Ultrasound may be ordered to check each baby's position. Expect to have blood work and an intravenous (IV) line placed in one arm. If a cesarean delivery is planned, the nurse inserts a urinary catheter into your bladder.

A vaginal examination is performed periodically to check the opening of the uterus. If the first twin's amniotic sac, also known as membranes or bag of waters, has already broken, an internal fetal monitor can be attached to the first twin in the birth canal to record that twin's response to labor. Otherwise, medical personnel might rupture the amniotic sac artificially, so they can attach an internal fetal monitor. A nurse secures an external fetal monitor on your abdomen to record the second twin's responses. (Two external monitors are used if the first twin's amniotic sac remains intact.)

Labor

Labor occurs in three stages. During the first stage the lower segment (cervix) of the uterus (womb) opens so that each twin's body can pass through it, one after the other, into the birth canal (vagina) for delivery. Since the cervix opens only once, you go through the first stage once. The second stage is the actual delivery of a baby, so it is repeated for each twin. During the third stage, the one large or two placentas are expelled. Almost always, both babies are born before either placenta is delivered.

Myth has it that labor always lasts longer for women carrying twins. This is not necessarily so. Mothers who have given birth before delivering twins report that their twin labors *tend* to follow their previous labor patterns. For some women, the overdistended twin uterus contracts less efficiently, which can prolong labor.

It is not uncommon to receive medication in the IV to induce or accelerate labor with twin births. This medication often causes more intense uterine contractions that peak more quickly. Discuss the reason for labor induction or acceleration with your doctor before you receive this medication.

Vaginal versus cesarean birth

According to a national hospital discharge survey, almost 60% of women that delivered twins had a cesarean delivery in 1989. Some obstetricians now routinely deliver twins by cesarean. However, research does not support routine surgical delivery as safer for twins when the first twin is vertex, or head first, in the birth canal, and the first twin is vertex about 80% of the time. The delivery route for your twins should be decided based on the circumstances surrounding your individual pregnancy and labor.

Labor support

Usually, your husband can stay with you throughout twin labor and vaginal or cesarean delivery. Because twin births are a special situation, consider taking an additional support person with you. This person, sometimes called a *doula*, can work with you, your husband, and the staff to see that your birth plans are carried out so you can concentrate on labor. To locate a trained support person or a doula service, ask your childbirth education instructor for suggestions.

Anesthesia options

Unmedicated labor and birth, sometimes called natural childbirth, is often possible with vaginal twin births. Some doctors and nurse midwives encourage this option because the mother can push more effectively during second-stage labor and forceps are not usually needed. This is especially beneficial for delivery of the second twin. Frequently, an episiotomy, an incision to enlarge the vaginal opening, is unnecessary. Though it does not happen often, the use of general anesthesia could become a necessity if there is any difficulty delivering the second twin. In such situations, there may be no time to administer an epidural or spinal anesthetic.

Epidural anesthesia is considered by many obstetricians to be the method of choice for many reasons: (1) it generally offers good pain relief during labor and delivery; (2) it can be used even if a cesarean delivery becomes necessary; and (3) you can sit to hold and nurse your babies after delivery. A possible disadvantage is that you may push less effectively during second-stage labor, so your doctor is more likely to need forceps to deliver one or both twins.

A spinal or saddle block is given immediately before delivery of the first baby or just before the beginning of a cesarean. It offers no relief during labor. You may be told to lie flat for several hours to prevent a spinal headache.

Delivery

The vaginal birth of the first twin is essentially the same as the birth of a single infant. The uterus often takes several minutes to rest after the first delivery and then readjusts around the second twin before second-stage contractions begin again. The position of the second twin cannot be determined absolutely until after the birth of the first twin. Occasionally, the doctor manipulates the position of the second twin to make delivery easier. Twins can be born several minutes to several hours apart. Time is not a problem as long as the second twin is monitored internally. The second twin is delivered quickly during a cesarean birth.

Expecting the unexpected

The most predictable thing about twin births is their unpredictability. All medical judgments concerning labor and birth should be discussed with you and your husband. You can relax and trust your obstetrician's decisions for your individual labor if you have been working together during pregnancy. (See Key 3.)

11

IMMEDIATE POSTPARTUM PERIOD

The immediate postpartum period is a time of great change, physically and emotionally. Your body shifts gears as it adapts to the babies' swift exit and prepares for lactation. Your mind works to integrate the pregnancy, labor, and birth experiences with the reality of your twins' arrival.

Physical changes

Vaginal bleeding is normal after a vaginal or a cesarean delivery.

1. You may bleed more the first day or two than a mother giving birth to one baby, since more of your uterus was covered by placental tissue.
2. Notify a nurse or your doctor whenever you fill more than two sanitary pads in an hour or pass a blood clot bigger than a golf ball.
3. Because it stretched to accommodate two babies, your uterus may not contract as well as it should. Check it several times a day. (It feels like a large grapefruit in the middle of your abdomen.) If your uterus does not feel hard or your bleeding increases, rub it until it contracts (hardens).
4. Afterbirth cramps (contractions) may be stronger after delivering twins. Also, you may feel stronger

menstrual-like cramps during early breastfeeding. You may be given medication having a similar effect if you bottlefeed your twins.

5. Bleeding often increases when new mothers try to accomplish too much. This is your body's way of saying, "Sit down and prop your feet up." Wear your robe for the first weeks after childbirth to remind yourself and others that you are still recuperating from a double delivery.

You may pass large amounts of urine and/or perspire excessively in the first days after childbirth. Your body is eliminating the extra blood volume it used during pregnancy.

Frequent breastfeedings initiated soon after birth are the best way to encourage breast milk production and avoid engorgement. Establish a pumping routine if initial breastfeeding must be delayed. (See Key 14.)

1. Insist that both twins be brought to you for all breastfeedings, including those at night.
2. If one twin cannot nurse, breastfeed the twin who can, and pump the other breast simultaneously. Most mothers express more milk this way.

Ask for a portable sitz bath. This warm water bath for your bottom encourages *episiotomy healing* and helps you feel more comfortable. This feels especially good if you experienced swelling and soreness in the pubic area during the last weeks of pregnancy, something very common with full-term twin pregnancies. Use your sitz bath at home after discharge from the hospital.

If you are among the many mothers of twins recuperating from a cesarean delivery, you have other comfort considerations.

1. New alternatives in postoperative pain relief allow you to begin to get up and to care for your twins the first day. The two more common alternatives are a one-time injection of a narcotic into the epidural anesthesia tubing for relief that lasts about 24 hours; or the release of small amounts of a narcotic medication slowly through an intravenous (IV) patient-controlled analgesia (PCA) pump. You control the button to release more medication into your system, but the pump does not let you overdose.

2. An oral form of pain medication is strong enough for most women 24 to 36 hours after delivery. Notify the nurse or your doctor if you do not get the pain relief you need.

3. Cushion the incision site with pillows when you hold and feed babies in your lap or turn in bed.

It may be a surprise to discover that your abdomen is not as flat when you stand as it first felt while lying on the delivery table:

1. Your body produced more of the hormone that loosens skin so your abdomen could stretch to accommodate two growing babies during pregnancy. This skin may feel loose for several months.

2. You have acquired "twinskin," or "seersucker skin," if your abdominal skin looks puckered. It lost some elasticity while stretching for a twin pregnancy. Twinskin is more common after delivering full-term, normal-birth-weight twins.

Emotional changes

You may have seen your twins on ultrasound many times, recognized their separate movements, and watched your abdomen overexpand as they grew inside you. Yet it may seem unbelievable that two babies could grow inside you until you meet them in person after delivery.

- You need to see and care for your twins together from birth so that the idea of two babies becomes physically real to you. Total or partial rooming-in makes this easier if twins are full term and in good physical condition.
- If one or both twins must be transferred to a newborn intensive care unit (NICU), ask someone to place your twins side by side so you can see them together before the transfer, unless it is an emergency. Take a photograph of them together if there is time. The birth of twins may seem less a reality if you are separated from either of them. (See Keys 12 and 24.)
- It is normal to want to know if your same-sex twins are identical or fraternal. It is as much a part of who twins are as eye color or other features. It is often impossible to determine twin type at birth. (See Key 22.)
- You may want to rehash the details of your twin pregnancy, labor, and birth with anyone who will listen. This is a necessary and normal aspect of organizing and integrating these special events in your memory.

Pregnancy lasts several months, and your body needs at least the same amount of time to get back to normal. Alhough physical and emotional change begins immediately after childbirth, the process of change continues throughout the postpartum year. Give yourself the gift of time. After all, two babies are a lot for the body and the mind to absorb.

12

~~~~~~

PREMATURITY

Many twins arrive before 36 weeks and weigh less than 5 pounds, 8 ounces. Yet you never thought this would happen to you. Your new bundles of joy are smaller than anticipated, and one or both may need to spend time in a newborn or neonatal intensive care unit (NICU). (See Key 4.)

Even if their conditions are stable, this is an unfamiliar and often frightening situation. If your babies have medical problems, you may experience incredible emotional highs and lows when the babies have dramatic positive and negative changes in their conditions. You may find yourself rejoicing in good news about one baby while anguishing over bad news concerning the other. To insulate yourself from the pain of possibly losing one, you may remain detached. Interaction and bonding are more difficult.

What to expect
- Until each twin is in stable condition and weighs about 5 pounds, they generally remain in the hospital. They may not be able to come home together.
- You may find it especially difficult to attach to one or both babies. Many mothers report feeling closer to the healthier twin. (See Key 24.)
- Sometimes a father feels closer to premature babies because he often must take control and begin visiting the NICU while mother recuperates from childbirth. If prematurity is coupled with what you consider to be a poor birth experience, you may experience feelings of inadequacy.

Suggestions

- Learn all you can about premature babies and their care. (See Appendix A: Suggested Reading on this subject.)

- Ask the nursery staff to place the twins' isolettes side-by-side so that visits are less complicated and to reinforce the reality that you gave birth to twins.

- Take pictures of the babies together and separately.

- Visit often. You and your babies need this contact.

- When you cannot visit, call frequently for updates. Ask about each baby separately.

- Call each baby by his or her given name. This makes twins seem more real.

- Do not refer to either baby as "the boy," "the smaller baby," or "the sicker baby." This may be a way of insulating and distancing yourself from the pain of having a sick baby.

- Concentrate on more than the twins' individual medical reports. Notice how each twin responds to being fed, changed, turned, or examined. What actions calm and which upset each twin?

- If a staff member refers to them as Baby A or Baby B or the twins, take the initiative and ask specific questions about Jimmy or Suzie.

- Leave something in each isolette that has your scent, such as a handkerchief or breast pad.

- No matter how premature your babies, beware the staggered homecoming. Many mothers report feeling closer to the twin who comes home first, usually responding first to that baby. If you are aware of this natural reaction, you can take steps to remedy the situation. (See Key 25.)

- Buy premie outfits. It is amazing how much better your babies look when they are dressed in something that fits! (See Appendix B: Resources.)

Feeding your premature babies

Many parents say they do not feel the babies are actually theirs until they begin to feed them, so ask to do this as soon as possible and keep asking. Do not let tubes and equipment get in the way of enjoying this nurturing experience. A nurse will show you how to hold your babies. Do not postpone contact with your babies until you are all home. You will gain confidence in handling twins if you begin early.

The breast milk of mothers who deliver prematurely is different from the breast milk of mothers who deliver full-term babies. It is perfect for your premature infants, so if you planned to breastfeed, do not give up now.

You need help if you decide to provide your babies with your milk. Call a local La Leche League leader or a certified lactation consultant immediately. They will coach you in how to nurse your premature babies and explain about breast pumps and transporting breast milk to the hospital. Most are willing to help you work with medical personnel. They can continue to offer advice and support when the babies come home. (See Appendix B: Resources.)

Whether they are fed by bottle or breast, premies need to eat more frequently than full-term babies. They usually take smaller amounts at each feeding, although it often takes them longer to feed.

Home

When you bring your babies home, expect to experience more anxiety than either the mother of full-term twins or the mother of a single baby born prematurely. These suggestions should help ease the transition:

• Get as much help as possible with household tasks so you can devote all your attention to your babies. Both you and they need it.

- Keep visitors to a minimum until you and the babies are stronger and you have established some kind of routine.
- During the day, keep them together where you can see them even while they sleep. This reinforces that you are now the parents of twins. If one awakens, even for a few moments, pick her up and cuddle only her. Your babies need contact with you even if they do not seem to crave it, and you need contact with them even if it does not feel natural at first.

Never blame yourself for your babies' premature birth. Guilt is unproductive. After a few months of worry you begin to relax and experience the trials and joys that all parents of twins experience. Remember that patience, determination, and an acceptance of your feelings as normal reactions to an unusual situation can overcome even the poorest beginning.

13

BREASTFEED OR BOTTLEFEED?

Choosing a feeding method for your twins is one of the biggest decisions you make. It is probably one of the most controversial as well. Possibly no other topic stimulates as much discussion as whether to feed by breast or bottle. Everyone has an opinion, and it is often based as much on emotion as fact. Remember, this is your special decision to make.

There is no question that "breast milk is best milk," yet generations of formula-fed babies successfully reached adulthood. Do not feel you are shortchanging your babies if you bottlefeed. Every mother, baby, and family is different. Only you can judge what is best in your situation. No matter which feeding method you choose, however, two babies *must* take more of your time and effort.

Feedings mean much more than food for both you and your infants. Not only do they meet your infants' physiological need for food, feedings also provide you, the primary care giver (usually the mother), with an opportunity to respond to each baby's cries, to hold each one close, and to interact while maintaining eye contact. These actions let a baby know he is loved. The love bond established between you and each infant enables each baby to feel safe, secure, and valued. Feeding interactions help you get to know both infants as individuals.

Feedings also show your infants that they can exert some control over their environment and trust it to meet their needs. (You are considered part of the environment.) Each learns this as he feels hunger and works up tension, often in the form of crying, trying to have this need met. When his cries are answered quickly, the infant discovers he can make things happen by communicating with the environment. He also comes to trust you, the consistent care giver, since you are the one who usually answers his cries by picking him up and feeding him to relieve hunger pangs.

If either one's cries (communications) are often ignored, the bottle (or breast) is frequently propped, or either is exposed to different care givers, he learns to think of himself as an inadequate signal sender. He begins to feel unworthy of being answered and cannot trust himself or his environment when his cries do not produce a predictable response.

Nature designed infant feedings as an activity to be repeated many times a day, giving you many opportunities to fulfill your infants' basic physiological and emotional needs. These two types of needs are equally important. Neither diminishes or disappears simply because an infant arrives as part of a set or because the chosen feeding method allows for propping the food supply or passing babies around to numerous care givers.

Your responsibility to meet each infant's *emotional* as well as physical needs does not change when you give birth to more than one baby. This is not to imply that no one else should ever help you feed your twins or that bottles should never be propped; in fact, doing either occasionally might better meet your babies' immediate needs. You must become particularly conscientious and not lose sight of your babies' emotional as well as physical needs in the reasonable quest for organization and efficiency.

Points to consider

Among the advantages of breastfeeding are:

- Breastfeeding ensures that you and your babies are in close contact many times a day, whether you are in the mood on a particular day or not! This provides opportunities for you to get to know each twin as an individual.
- Breast milk is nutritionally superior.
- Breast milk contains antibodies and anti-allergic factors that cannot be duplicated in artificial formulas. This is helpful in avoiding illness with twins who often share contagious diseases.
- Breastfeeding is more economical. The extra calories you need cost much less than formula, and no expensive equipment is required.
- Breastfeeding requires no preparation, refrigeration or clean up. It is always available and is at the right temperature.
- Many mothers say the frequent feedings give them an excuse to sit and rest during the day.

The advantages of bottlefeeding twins include:

- Each parent can feed and concentrate totally on one baby. This affords both parents good opportunities to discover their infants as individuals.
- Fathers have more opportunity to become involved in the feeding process—a necessary and pleasant part of caring for an infant.
- Dad or someone else can take over feeding during all or part of the night, giving Mom time to recoup her strength after childbirth or after a few nights "on call" herself.
- You have more energy to offer your babies the next day after a good night's rest. (See Key 32.)
- Your personality may dictate knowing exactly how much

nourishment your babies are getting and formula can be measured.

• If you leave your twins with a sitter, you know their need for food can be easily met and they are more likely to be content in your absence.

Suggestions regardless of method

It is very easy to allow feedings and other infant care needs to become too task-oriented and inflexibly organized when caring for two newborns. Only you can ensure that this does not happen.

Mothers of newborn twins describe their lives as "just one feeding after another." If this is to be your life for awhile, find a way to enjoy it. During this early period you and each infant establish patterns of relating to one another.

Infant feedings play a critical role in laying the foundation for patterns that continue long after you and your twins move on to other stages of development.

14

BREASTFEEDING
TWINS

Nature designed your body so that you can breastfeed as many babies as your pregnancy produces. Ignore those who say, "You can't possibly make enough milk for two babies," or "It will be too hard on you and your family to try to nurse twins." You *can* breastfeed no matter what the circumstances. If a stress-free newborn period was a requirement for success, few mothers of twins could meet it!

Breastfeeding twins requires an understanding of breast milk production, a commitment to continue through the early adjustment period, and an available support network. Once you separate twin issues from breastfeeding issues, you may discover that breastfeeding is the least complicated aspect of caring for two.

Getting started

Early, frequent feedings begun soon after birth are the best way to promote double milk production. When babies require a stay in a special care nursery, simulate Nature's plan by pumping your breasts 8 to 12 times a day. (See Keys 11 and 12.)

Allow both twins to breastfeed on demand for several weeks. Human milk production operates on the principle of supply and demand, so the more each baby nurses, the more breast milk you produce. Demand feedings are your twins' way of telling your body how much milk to make.

Schedules (will you settle for routines?)

Some babies regularly space breastfeedings two to three hours apart; others sleep for longer periods and then "bunch" several feedings close together. Both patterns are normal. Generally, fairly predictable feeding routines evolve by six to eight weeks.

- You can continue breastfeeding twins on demand. By letting each twin set the pace, you appreciate both as individuals with changing needs.
- If you require a more defined schedule to physically manage double feedings, schedule feedings by waking one twin to nurse just before, with, or after the other.
- Scheduled and demand feedings can be combined. Try scheduling feeding during the day, but nurse on demand during the night in case one twin is ready to stretch a sleep cycle. Or feed your twins on demand for true "meals," but offer pacifiers afterward for nonnutritive sucking.

Never "put off" either twin to reach some ideal number of hours between feedings. To do so interferes with milk production and babies' weight gains.

Coordinating double breastfeedings

Almost any method of coordinating double feedings works, as long as each twin breastfeeds at least eight to twelve times in 24 hours. The following are the most common methods of coordinating breastfeedings.

- The simplest routine is to offer each twin one breast per feeding and alternate babies and breasts every 24 hours. Assign the right breast to one twin and the left breast to the other twin one day and switch them the following day.
- Offer both breasts to each baby at every feeding. For example, Baby A begins nursing at your right breast for 10 to 15

minutes and finishes the feeding on the left. Baby B nurses on the left breast before finishing on the right.

- You could assign each baby a specific breast for all feedings. You might have a problem, though, if one twin cannot nurse for a few days and the second twin is unwilling to nurse on the other side. Also, your breasts' sizes may be noticeably different if one twin has a bigger appetite. If you use this method, alternate feeding positions so that both eyes of each baby receive adequate visual stimulation.

Simultaneous versus separate feedings

Simultaneous breastfeedings, nursing twins together, is the most efficient and effective way of handling double feedings. However, you may desire the closeness of separately nursing each baby. Most mothers *combine* methods and nurse twins together for some feedings and separately for others.

Your twins influence this feeding decision. Their sleep-wake patterns play a role. Also, one twin may refuse to cooperate with simultaneous feedings, but another will not nurse unless the second twin nurses. Some babies have difficulty with simultaneous feedings in the early weeks but do well when they are a bit older.

Experiment with simultaneous nursing positions (See illustrations page 51.) Place pillows across your lap and under your arms as extra arms to prop, support, and hold infants in position. The most common simultaneous feeding positions are the following:

- *The double cradle hold:* Support a baby's head in the crook of each arm and crisscross their bodies in front of you or lay each along one of your thighs.
- *The football or clutch hold:* Supporting the back of a baby's head in each of your hands, tuck one of the babies' bodies under each arm—along or away from the side of your body.

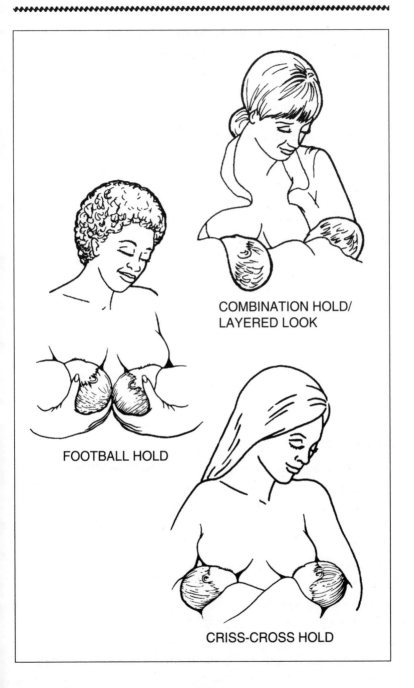

COMBINATION HOLD/
LAYERED LOOK

FOOTBALL HOLD

CRISS-CROSS HOLD

• *The combination hold:* Hold the first twin in the cradle position. Place the second in the clutch hold with his head gently laying on the first twin's abdomen. Mothers prefer this position for babies who have difficulty latching on, plus it lends itself to more discreet nursing.

Most other simultaneous feeding positions are variations of these three basic holds. Adapt these positions to nurse while lying down or sitting in a recliner chair.

See Key 21 for ideas on support and Appendices A and B for a list of books and agencies with more detailed information about breastfeeding.

15

~~~~~~

BOTTLEFEEDING TWINS

You can bottlefeed your twins on demand or on schedule. Some babies adapt easily to a schedule that coincides with the parents' life-style; others manage better if they can set their own schedules. Sometimes parents allow one twin to set the schedule for both. (If one baby needs to be fed, then both are fed even if it means waking the other.) What works today may need to be adjusted tomorrow, so be flexible.

Preparation

Bottles, nipples, and formula should be purchased or borrowed and sterilized before your babies' birth. Create a simple chart to post on the refrigerator or their cribs to record the amount each baby consumes at each feeding, who is fed when, and you are ready for their arrival.

Cost versus convenience

Infants' nourishment is too important for you to experiment. The babies' doctor should have the final word on the formula you use. Most formulas come in three different forms: ready to feed, concentrate, and powdered. The form you choose should balance convenience and cost.

"Ready to feed" formula is the most convenient. You simply open a can, pour the formula into a bottle, and feed your babies. It is also the most expensive.

Concentrate is easy to use and is a little less expensive. Mix concentrate with boiled or distilled water and refrigerate both the formula and any unused concentrate.

Powdered formula is the least expensive. It is not refrigerated until mixed with water. It is convenient for travel because you can carry the powder and water separately and unrefrigerated, not mixing until you need to feed the babies. Some powdered formulas are missing an essential fat that is contained in their liquid counterparts. Ask your babies' doctor about this. Also, if the powder does not dissolve completely, it clogs the nipples.

Bottles

You have numerous choices when selecting bottles and nipples. If your babies have difficulty with the nipples you select, try another type or brand.

Color code the bottles or caps for each baby. If Suzie gets the pink bottles, give Johnny the blue. You then know how much each twin is eating, which bottle to grab, and which twin was fed last.

If your twins were premature, consider using premie nipples for the first few weeks. They are smaller and softer than standard nipples, and your babies do not have to work as hard to get formula.

Feeding

Feeding one twin alone while the other is pleasantly occupied is an ideal situation since it gives you time for one-on-one interaction with each baby. If your twins readily adjust to a schedule, one baby should be sleeping or happy in a swing while you feed the other.

Of course, this does not always happen! If you have help with feedings, alternate which twin you feed even if one of your babies accepts another care giver more readily. It is important for you to experience one-on-one closeness with each baby. This rotation should include those feedings accomplished by both parents. One father always grabbed the baby who ate faster and spit up less. He stopped when he realized that he felt closer to the twin he always fed.

Joint feedings

Feeding your twins together is an exciting experience. Take turns establishing eye contact with each baby. Call each by name as you become part of a love triangle. As the babies share you, you witness the love that exists between them as well as between you and each of them.

Joint feeding becomes easier as your twins grow older. You soon find a position that suits you, your babies, and your circumstances. These are some of the most common ways of feeding two babies together:

- You and your infant twins can be close and more comfortable if you feed them while you sit in bed, on a sofa, or in a large chair and the babies rest on pillows alongside your body.
- Place each twin in an infant seat, sit between the babies holding a bottle in each hand, and lay one of your arms along the body of each baby while they feed. Take turns looking at and burping each baby. If infant seats seem unstable, try using walkers with reclining seats. These are generally very sturdy.
- Use pillows and furniture. Hold and feed one baby while the other lays beside you on a couch with her bottle propped against your leg.
- If your babies need to burp often, try propping both bottles initially and take turns burping each twin. This gives you the freedom to quickly pick up the twin who needs you. To

prop bottles use small blankets, towels, or clean diapers rolled up or you can purchase bottle proppers.

Never leave an infant unattended with a propped bottle. Infants choke easily. You prop bottles so your babies are more comfortable, not to give you free time. Do not be lulled into a false sense of security because you have propped bottles for weeks and "nothing has ever happened." It only takes one time!

• As your babies gain strength, sit on the floor with their heads resting on your outstretched left leg and their bodies between your legs. While you hold the bottles in your right hand stroke the babies' heads with your left hand. This position lets your twins cuddle with each other, something they often find both fun and comforting.

Not just a routine

If this is to be your life, find a way to enjoy it. Make the most of each feeding. Consider each meal another opportunity to get to know and love your babies.

16

COMBINING BREAST AND BOTTLE

You may wonder if you can combine breast and bottle-feeding. The answer is a qualified "yes." Offering complementary bottles can be compatible with continued breastfeeding. Giving frequent supplements or alternating methods half the time rarely works. The keys to a realistic feeding plan that combines methods are an understanding of how your breastfeeding body works and the trade-offs involved.

Whenever your twins breastfeed, they signal your body to increase milk production. No signals are sent when either twin bottlefeeds, so your body cuts back on production. Giving too many bottles, particularly during the early months, *significantly* decreases breast milk production and leads to early weaning.

There are trade-offs if you combine your milk with formula. The antibody and anti-allergic properties of breast milk are increasingly less effective as more formula is given, but statistically even partially breastfed infants have fewer illnesses in the first year than their bottlefed counterparts.

Why combine?

When many twins are discharged from the hospital, they are taking formula because they had poor breastfeeding starts related to prematurity, delivery complications, and/or early mismanagement of breastfeeding. It may be more difficult to overcome a poor start while caring for two babies, or you might continue including bottles because you do not know how to eliminate them.

You may choose to offer bottles for different reasons. You may think you do not have enough milk for both twins. Because of other responsibilities there may not be enough hours in a day for double breastfeedings, or you might simply want help with some feedings. Perhaps one or both twins need a boost after an inadequate weight gain. Also, you need to leave bottles if your twins are in someone else's care.

Increasing breast milk production

To make up for lost time after a slow start, a few days of around-the-clock breastfeeding is usually enough to increase milk production. If this sounds overwhelming or you must ease the transition from bottle to breast, breastfeed on demand and begin to delete ½ to 1 ounce of formula per bottle per day for several days. Plan on more frequent breastfeedings until milk production increases. Once each twin falls into an 8 to 12 feedings a day routine, delete another ½ to 1 ounce per bottle per day. Repeat this pattern until you reach your desired goal. (See Key 14.)

Are they getting enough?

You may wonder if you are making enough milk for twins since your breasts are not designed with windows and ounce markers. Ask yourself if, in 24 hours of exclusive breastfeeding, is each twin usually (1) satisfied with eight to twelve feedings; (2) soaking 6 to 10 diapers; and (3) having several loose bowel movements? Is each gaining 4 to 8 ounces a week? If so, you have plenty of milk!

Planning ahead

When you have the option, do not introduce bottles or formula until your milk production is well established after three to four weeks of exclusive breastfeeding. By this time your babies have learned how to latch onto and remove milk from your breasts. Some newborns become nipple-confused and have more difficulty latching onto the breast if they receive bottles in the early weeks. This adds time and frustration to double breastfeedings. If you think either twin suffers from nipple confusion, you need extra support. (See Key 21 and Appendix B for more information.)

Realistic combinations

Breast- and bottle-feeding combinations should interfere as little as possible with breast milk production. This is a situation in which less is more, so think complement rather than supplement. A *complement* is 1 or 2 ounces of expressed breast milk or formula given after and in addition to a breastfeeding. A *supplement* takes the place of a breastfeeding.

- Offering a complement after one or two breastfeedings in the evening or during the night appears to have the least effect on milk production. Milk supply often seems lower at night and father may be available to participate in feedings. Also, this is enough to accustom your babies to bottles should you ever miss a feeding.
- Complementing every breastfeeding is rarely necessary even to boost either twin's weight gain. It is time consuming and results in a decrease in breast milk production.
- One supplement should not hurt milk production if each twin nurses at *least* seven or eight times a day.

Avoid alternating

Alternating breast and bottle may seem the perfect solution, but actually it combines the disadvantages of both methods. Early weaning from the breast is common because milk production lowers, the incidence of nipple confusion increases, and it is too much work.

Alternation generally takes one of two forms: (1) nurse one twin and supplement the other at each feeding, alternating which twin receives the breast and which the bottle; or (2) offer the breast to both twins for one feeding and supplement both at the next. With either form, you invest the time and effort needed to totally breastfeed and totally bottlefeed.

Exclusively breastfeeding only one twin and bottlefeeding the other is a poor idea. It can affect your relationship with each baby. This should be undertaken only in extremely rare circumstances.

Successful breastfeeding

Exclusive breastfeeding is nature's ideal, but breastfeeding does not have to be all or nothing. Infant formula was manufactured originally for special situations, and caring for twins is definitely in that category. Although many mothers exclusively breastfeed twins for several months, every family is unique. Only you can judge your situation. Both you and your twins benefit no matter what the amount or duration of your shared breastfeeding experience.

17

MOTHER FEELINGS

Your babies are here and you still are not quite sure how you feel or how you *should* feel. Many outside influences have an impact on your initial feelings for your babies. Were your twins born prematurely? Did you have an emergency cesarean? Was your support during labor and delivery all you expected and needed? Did you have the labor and delivery of your dreams?

The first few weeks or even months after your babies' births, postpartum changes can wreak havoc with your emotions. Your body has not returned to normal, and you may wonder if it ever will. The babies have become the center of attention instead of you. You may feel overwhelmed by the responsibility of parenting these two small babies, yet reluctant to hand over any of their care to someone else, even their father. You may feel a heightened sense of possessiveness of your twins, you may feel distant from them, or you may even feel both ways. Relax. All these feelings are normal.

Recovering from a twin pregnancy and delivery is harder on your body and your emotions than a single pregnancy and birth. An exaggerated healing process places huge demands on you, both physically and emotionally, as you care for your expanded family.

Humans crave predictable patterns in their lives. Continuity gives reassurance and comfort. The birth of twins necessitates the development of a new pattern. Until that pattern emerges and you integrate it into your lives you may feel disoriented and unsure. There is no set time frame for this. Do not judge yourself negatively if, at first, you have ambivalent feelings about your new situation.

Your body probably has not returned to normal, and it is unrealistic to expect it to snap right back. It took months to get out of shape, so give yourself months to regain it. Added weight, stretch marks, and loose skin can change the image you have of yourself. You may wonder if your husband finds you unattractive. Exercise and wearing clothing that camouflages the bulges will help while your body returns to normal. Make time for yourself. Snatching little bits of time is more realistic for now, but they add up. Spend them in ways you like. (See Key 11.)

As the reality of being the mother of twins sets in, you may experience intense emotions of wonder, joy, and excitement as you look at them lying side by side. This feeling of awe resurfaces many times as they grow.

You may feel closer to one twin or the other for a variety of reasons. Do not deny these feelings if they exist. Instead, work through them. You may have to force yourself to relate and respond to both babies. (See Key 25.)

You will experience tremendous highs and lows as you care for and learn to know your twins. On a good day when everything goes according to plan, you may feel superior to and certainly luckier than everyone. On a bad day, when nothing seems to be working, you may feel inadequate, out of control, and wonder why you were sent two babies at once.

You probably are vulnerable to other people's comments or opinions of your mothering style. Learn to listen to your heart. Accept and love each twin, other family members, and yourself for who each is.

18

FATHER FEELINGS

Surveys indicate that after the initial shock and excitement of the discovery of a twin pregnancy, you may worry about increased financial obligations. As your wife's pregnancy progresses, you may feel anxious about the health of your wife and babies. Becoming involved is the best reassurance. Accompany your wife to the doctor and for her sonograms. Ask questions. Be supportive. She is concerned, too, and appreciates your involvement.

Bonding begins as soon as you learn you are having twins. Visualize your new babies. Begin to let the reality of twins set in.

Your wife and older children need your attention, help, and support during this pregnancy and after your twins are born. Your wife probably will not be able to keep up her prepregnancy pace. Offer to take over some of her chores. Pay extra attention to your older children, so they will not feel left out.

You may expect life to return to normal shortly after the babies arrive. A new "normal" life emerges, but it cannot be what it was before. Your family has expanded by two instead of the customary one, and it is going to be different. In the long run, it is better, but it takes time to adjust. (See Key 28.)

Many fathers take a more active role caring for infant twins than they would for a single child. They view this as a very positive experience.

"One of the nicest things about having twins," said one father, "is knowing they need me to care for them, too. My wife could handle our single infant by herself."

Most mothers develop an organized system to cope with twins. It will not include you if you are not home much. If this happens, insert yourself into her plan whenever you are available. Do not wait for your wife to ask for help. It is not that your wife consciously leaves you out, she simply has learned to cope and needs a reminder when you are there.

Having twins gives you a fantastic opportunity to stretch your role as a father. For instance, older children need reassuring that they are important. Their need for attention increases while their mother's time for them decreases. At the same time, each twin needs as much cuddling as a single baby. You, their father, can provide the extra arms for loving, cuddling, feeding, bathing, rocking, and walking.

Be the one to tie up loose household ends. Your wife will appreciate help with any kind of housekeeping. Take over a number of routine chores, such as grocery shopping or the laundry. The important thing is that you take over not only the actual task, but also the responsibility for completing it.

The lives of other new parents may seem to return to normal long before yours. Do not be discouraged. They are only making the adjustment to the birth of one baby. You and your family are adjusting to two. It is a wonderful and unique, but abnormal, situation. Those with "normal situations" never experience the thrill of watching twins grow up.

19

FINDING TIME TO
BE A COUPLE

The birth of twins changes the dynamics of a family. Many couples are unprepared for the changes within their relationship that accompanies the birth of two babies. Everyone responds to change, stress, lack of sleep, and possibly inadequate nutrition in a unique way. You cannot plan your response to this situation.

One very important dynamic for any family is the relationship between mother and father. In all your planning for twins, you may ignore yourselves as a couple. You may think that this "couple" relationship miraculously returns to "normal" within a few weeks of your twins' birth, but this is usually an unrealistic expectation.

Caring for two babies requires a tremendous amount of time. It can be physically and emotionally all-consuming for both parents. So much is happening every day that your relationship as a couple seems lost in the shuffle. Fathers generally become aware of this loss sooner than mothers because their bodies and emotions have not been upset by pregnancy and birth and few fathers are the primary care giver.

Keep the following in mind when you evaluate where you think you are in your relationship. These should help to place any negative feelings into perspective:

- It takes a mother longer to recover from a twin pregnancy and childbirth. This is especially true if you have a cesarean delivery.

- A mother who spends all day caring for babies and young children often feels "touched out." She is in physical contact with at least one other human for most of the day and may not appreciate more contact or lovemaking with her spouse at the end of the day.
- Men's physical drives and needs change little with the birth of twins. Their bodies have not gone through huge changes. They return to work and an accustomed daily routine in a short period of time.
- Many husbands have an intense need to interact and make love to their wives as they did before the twins were born. Both partners must compromise to meet each other's physical and emotional needs. For example, making love on the same timetable and with the same abandon as before the twins were born is unrealistic.
- Physical and emotional needs differ from individual to individual and from couple to couple. Do not compare each other or yourselves as a couple with anyone else. Do what is right for you.

Communication is the key to a happy marriage after the birth of twins. Each parent must make his or her needs known to the other. Your time is limited, so be creative in showing your partner that he or she is still important. The following suggestions have all been used by other parents of twins.

- Say, "I love you," often. This takes almost no energy and can be said anytime.
- Go out of your way once each day to do something considerate for the other. One new mother woke her husband every day and gave him his morning coffee and paper in bed. No matter what happened the rest of the day, he felt loved. He took charge of washing the diapers. This may

sound less romantic, but she said that his performing such a thankless chore was a definite affirmation of his love for her.

- Assume nothing. Say what you mean in a nonthreatening way. Tell your spouse how you feel. Each of you may be too tired or too busy to pick up on nonverbal communications.
- Take walks together, or eat dinner by candlelight even if each of you holds a baby.
- Make dates with each other, and look forward to the time you spend together.
- Give each other time away alone. Agree to be the one to get up with the babies during the night to ensure that your partner gets a full night's sleep. Mothers especially may appreciate these considerations.
- Be creative with your lovemaking. Forget past notions of the proper time or place. Exhausted parents of twins are rarely in the mood late in the evening. Make an appointment with each other for early in the morning, or hire a sitter to take the children for a walk. Even a "quickie" says, "I love you."

New parents often wonder if there is life after having twins. The twins seem all-consuming at first, but there is definitely life after twins and it is even more special because of the sensitivity you show one another.

20

SIBLING ADJUSTMENT

L ook at life for the family of newborn twins from the perspective of an older sibling. Not one baby, but two have come to displace her as the center of her mother's and father's world. Relatives and friends visit, and in their haste to see the twins, they often ignore her. Strangers on the street inch her aside to ogle the twins in their stroller. People used to tell her *she* was beautiful; now they tell her how lucky she is to have twin siblings.

She is not feeling lucky. Two babies cry a lot. Her mother is always tired. Just when she has her mother's undivided attention, a baby needs to be fed or changed. Instead of reading her a story when he comes home from work, her father cares for the babies so her mother can fix dinner. "Wait a minute" suddenly becomes her parents' favorite response to any request.

You want and need to nurture all your children, not only your twins. Coming home with two babies instead of one does not change the needs of an older child. Fortunately, there are ways to ensure their position as important members of the family. These thoughts and suggestions may be helpful in dealing with your older children:

- Acknowledge your child's negative feelings. Let him know you understand his frustrations.
- Talk to your older children about when they were babies. Tell them how much time you spent taking care of them. Show them photos and videos of themselves as babies.
- As a parent of twins, you feel special. This specialness

rarely extends to other children. Explain to your older children that two babies take extra time and attention. It is not that twins are more special.

- Spend some uninterrupted time with each of your older children each day. You might arrange to do this during the twins' nap time, or hire a baby-sitter to take the twins for a walk.

- *Regression* is a child's natural reaction to a dramatic change in routine. Do not make a big deal of it, but emphasize the privileges of being a "big kid."

- You may not be able to control strangers, but you can direct friends and relatives to pay attention to your older children.

- When you are out, try placing one of the twins in an infant carrier and allow an older sibling to ride in the twin stroller. This makes the sibling feel special and you are less likely to be stopped by strangers who want to look at the twins.

- Help your children appreciate their place within the family structure as older siblings. Fathers, especially, should spend time with older children doing fun things. Mention occasionally to each child that you appreciate your time together. You might also point out that you can do certain things together because they are older.

- Have realistic expectations of older children. You sometimes may be so desperate for help that even the youngest older sibling is seen as a kind of mother's helper. Different children's interest in helping with babies varies. Some love it, but some are apathetic. Children have short attention spans.

- If you do not want to create negative feelings, do not blame the twins for everything that you no longer can do. If you used to go to the pool every day but can only make it once a week now, your older children do not need to be reminded that the twins are the reason.

- Let older children, even toddlers, know that you sometimes feel overwhelmed with all you have to do. They appreciate knowing your feelings and that you are are human, too.
- When your twins reach the toddler stage, expect new feelings of frustration from older children. Once twins are mobile, they disturb their siblings' life-style because toddlers, by nature, get into everything. Older children, by nature, do not put anything away! Give older children their own space. Place sliding locks on the bedroom doors, so their things are safe from toddler twins.

Each of your children will react to the birth of twins in a different way. Some siblings seem to bask in the glow of the family's twins at first, but may express resentment later. As parents you need to be aware of possible negative feelings and prepare yourself to deal with them as part of a natural growth process for your children.

Siblings often differentiate between twins before their parents, often preferring one twin more than the other at first. As they grow, single siblings easily develop a separate relationship with each twin.

Growth experience

Siblings' lives change greatly with the birth of twins. As they learn to do things on their own they experience growth in self-confidence. Each has a special place within the family unit, and you have the responsibility of reaffirming the importance of this position.

21

SUPPORT

Sharing experiences with someone in the same position provides tremendous emotional support whether you are a mother, father, or sibling of twins. You are in a unique situation, experiencing special joys, concerns, and feelings. Only someone who has experienced or is experiencing the same situation can understand both your positive and negative feelings.

The mother, as the primary care giver, is particularly vulnerable to feelings of isolation. Generally, she is the one who is expected to maintain the family's emotional well-being. It is difficult to do this in a vacuum.

This is the time to aggressively look for and establish new relationships. Contact your local Mothers of Twins Club. Most have monthly business meetings, with a guest speaker, followed by social time for mothers only. Many include used clothing sales, special "mother's night out" parties, family get-togethers, and holiday celebrations as part of their services.

Even if you cannot attend meetings, consider the Mothers of Twins Club as a resource. Call an officer. Ask that a member with a similar family situation call you. You will have plenty to talk about.

Ask your obstetrician or pediatrician for the names of other mothers of twins who might welcome a call. Mutual friends may know other mothers of twins. Everyone seems to know someone who has twins.

The twins themselves are wonderful icebreakers. Two mothers became best friends after introducing themselves at the mall while each strolled with twins. One mother was so desperate for companionship that she knocked on a stranger's door after observing twins playing in the yard. They became immediate "best friends" and have maintained that relationship for almost 20 years.

If you are a nursing mother, contact La Leche League International. They can provide you with names and phone numbers of leaders who have breastfed twins and of the leader who lives closest to you. Someone who has breastfed twins will be able to bolster your self-confidence and help you maintain perspective during your twins' early months of frequent breastfeeding, and the local leader can help with basic information.

Do not forget other members of the family. They too can benefit from a support system, understanding, and camaraderie. An older sibling who is feeling displaced by the birth of twins may feel less hurt having a friend who feels the same way. Depending on the children's ages and their mood at the moment, they may share feelings of pride in the twins or frustration at the twins' intrusion into their lives. Sometimes older siblings of twins from different familes "adopt" each other and pretend they too are twins. The significance of this game can be appreciated only by siblings of twins.

A new father might appreciate hearing another dad confirm his feelings. The father's needs are often considered *after* those of the babies, mother, and older siblings. Remember, he too is adjusting to a new situation. Whether he is a first-time father or his twins were born after other children, their birth has a tremendous impact on his life and his lifestyle. Even sharing "twin stories" with a casual friend occasionally eases tension or feelings of isolation.

A family might also benefit from professional counseling in addition to talking with other families with twins. This is particularly true if you are coping with other stressful situations while caring for young twins. Sometimes a counselor has a perspective that helps in special situations. If you think you need extra help, you probably do.

The "buddy" system provides a fantastic positive experience for parents of twins. Sharing your emotional highs with someone who understands is as important as sharing any lows. No one but another parent of twins can fully appreciate the thrill you experience as you cradle your two babies or watch your twin toddlers interact.

22

DETERMINING TWIN TYPE

There are both physical and emotional reasons for wanting to know if your twins are identical or fraternal. Their twin type is, after all, a part of who each is. Also, you may need to know if your twins are identical or fraternal for medical reasons.

Evidence of twin type

Sometimes the determination of twin type is straightforward. You know twins are *fraternal* if they are opposite sexes, each has a different blood type, one is totally bald and the other has a full head of hair, or their hair colors are completely different. You can be certain they are *identical* if an examination of the one placenta reveals a single chorion.

A definite diagnosis of twin type is not always possible. Informal surveys that we have conducted indicate that 15 to 25% of parents are not sure whether their twins are identical or fraternal. Many were given a determination of twin type after the twins' birth, but they doubt the classification.

Factors sometimes used to help determine twin type may not be accurate. The size and shape of the twins' heads, their weights, their lengths, and their skin color at birth are not indicative of twin type. Exposure to environmental situations during pregnancy and birth and shortly after birth can be responsible for differences in any of these factors.

Most identical twins share one placenta, yet 25% of identical twins have separate placentas. Some health professionals are unaware of this. Many twins have been inaccurately typed as fraternal because the only basis for diagnosis was the presence of two placentas.

If you are unsure whether your babies are fraternal or identical, look for further evidence to establish twin type as they grow.

Identical twins have the same:

1. Blood type and subtypes;
2. Eye color;
3. Hair color and texture;
4. Facial features and ear shape;
5. Body build;
6. Often similar mannerisms; and;
7. Generally quite close patterns of physical and mental growth and development unless either sustained a pregnancy or delivery-related impairment.

It is impossible for any other two siblings to have so many physical and developmental characteristics in common.

Another clue to twin type is other people's reactions. Identical twins are frequently confused even by friends and relatives who see them often. Do you ever have difficulty telling your twins apart while they sleep, although you easily know who is who when either is awake? Without their personalities enlivening their features, identical twins look more alike.

Scientific determination of twin type

Informal evidence may not be enough when fraternal twins share the maximum number of genes possible for siblings. If you still wonder what type of twins you have, two laboratory tests are available that accurately ascertain twin type. These are blood subtyping and genetic "fingerprinting," or banding.

When most people discuss blood type, they mean the major type—A, B, or O. Each person also has many blood subtypes. Fraternal twins may share the same major blood type and Rh (rhesus) factor, but differences should be apparent when blood is tested for subtypes. Very few fraternal twin sets have all subtypes in common.

Genetic banding, or *genetic fingerprinting*, is a method for examining someone's DNA, the carrier of each person's unique genetic code. The DNA of each of us creates a unique banding pattern. The DNA banding patterns of two siblings show more resemblance than that for two strangers, but only with identical twins is the pattern in a set of chromosomes almost identical. Blood is frequently used as a sample for this test, but any human tissue may be sent to a laboratory for testing.

Testing blood subtypes is slightly less foolproof than genetic banding. It can be done at most medical laboratories, but genetic banding is available only in certain medical centers. Unfortunately, laboratory tests usually costs several hundred dollars for both twins and insurance rarely covers this expense. Essentially, accurate twin type determination is a luxury that many families cannot afford. It is reassuring to know technology is available if you need to know twin type at some point in the future. It is a shame that twins and their parents do not have access to this information.

The need to know

Being an identical or fraternal twin is a part of each twin's identity, a significant part of who either is. Do not let anyone tell you that it is not important. If you or your twins want to know, then it is important.

23

GETTING TO
KNOW TWO

The word *bonding* has become synonymous with the idea of an "instant glue" that mysteriously cements a parent and newborn during a magical moment soon after birth. Bonding is actually the formation of an enduring attachment between parent and baby. This ongoing process of "falling in love" with an infant begins during pregnancy and continues after delivery. Usually, a parent falls in love with only one infant at a time. With twins, you *must* fall in love with two persons at once.

Your interactions with each twin create the foundation for each one's sense of self. The process of attachment is intricately woven with the formation of a separate identity for a twin. As you develop a strong, separate attachment to each baby, you cannot help but get to know and treat each twin as an individual. Young twins realize during toddlerhood or preschool age whether each is loved and held in esteem as individuals, or is valued more as half of a whole set.

A different process

Learning to love two babies simultaneously is quite a different process from bonding with a single infant. Forming a separate attachment with each individual twin takes months or even years longer than it does for a parent with a single baby.

There are many reasons for the longer attachment process with twins. Also, several factors often complicate the process. The early, extended contact with babies that enhances initial feelings of attachment is less likely to occur after a multiple birth. Prematurity and other complications of pregnancy or delivery leading to parent-infant separation from one or both twins are extremely common. Even when birth and early postpartum conditions are ideal, it can be difficult at first to relate to each twin separately. (See Key 4.)

All parents have a prenatal fantasy baby that must be reconciled with the "real" baby when forming an attachment with a single infant. Prenatal fantasies are multiplied when expecting twins. Think about your prenatal fantasy life. Did you prefer identical or fraternal twins? If you envisioned same-sex twins, were the babies a particular sex? Did opposite-sex twins seem more appealing? How alike or different did your babies look in prebirth fantasies? Perhaps you visualized life with easygoing, placid twins only to find yourself with two babies who have different minds of their own.

Obviously, getting to know and accept the two complicated little persons you actually delivered rather than the ones you imagined takes time. Time, or the lack of it, is a major factor in a prolonged attachment process. Quiet periods to enjoy one twin alone are usually few and far between. It is also easy to miss opportunities to seize a few moments with only one baby when riding a dizzying baby care merry-go-round.

Considerations

Forming a separate attachment with each twin is critical no matter how prolonged the process. Each infant's physical and emotional survival hinges on the development of an enduring attachment with you. The twin-twin relationship can never replace each parent-child relationship. Besides each twin's need for a relationship with you, you also have a need to feel a deep bond with each of your children. After all, the relationships established with your children are the true rewards of child rearing.

Most parents form a strong, separate attachment with each twin, so relax. Do not worry that you and your twins must go through life without bonding if

1. You happen to miss early, extended contact;
2. You were separated from one or both after birth, or;
3. Now that you are home you have little time to interact with two babies.

Give yourself and your babies all the time you need to get to know one another.

24

THE TWIN BONDING PROCESS

Parents of twins generally begin forming separate attachments with each twin in one of two ways. You may begin to feel an attachment with one twin before the other, or you might feel close to your twins as a unit before forming an attachment to them as individuals.

Preferential treatment

Certain situations are conducive to bonding more closely with one twin than the other.

When one premature or ill twin responds to you earlier than the other; one is separated from you in a newborn intensive care unit (NICU) while you care for the other in your hospital room; or one twin is discharged from the NICU before the other, you are likely to feel an initial closeness to the infant who first responds to you or who is first in your care. (See Key 45.)

- Often the twin who responds first and the one first in your care is the same baby.
- Many mothers say they quickly become attached to the twin constantly in their care, while fathers spend more time with and feel closer to the twin in the intensive care unit.
- Occasionally, a separated parent feels a psychic bond with the twin in the NICU and begins to form a closer attachment with the twin not in her care.
- The first-born twin is more likely to receive preferential

treatment. The second-born twin is generally the smaller infant and the one more likely to suffer from complications requiring special care.

- The second-born twin is also the "unexpected bonus" if twins are undiagnosed until labor or birth. One mother describing her unanticipated twin birth said, "For a long time I thought of the firstborn twin as 'my' baby. She was the baby I imagined during pregnancy. It was quite awhile before I could think of the second-born 'surprise' as anything other than an intruder."

- Some parents feel closer to the "underdog" twin, the one that others are less attracted to for whatever reason. The underdog is often the twin who demands more attention, so you are forced to take time to interact with this twin. Chances are you have had more opportunity to get to know and appreciate this twin's special qualities.

- Opposite-sex twins present a different scenario. It is natural to feel drawn toward and interact more with the twin of the sex you had hoped for.

- If one twin is born with some type of disability or physical condition, your feelings might be unequal. Often the "perfect" twin is also the one who is not separated or responds more, which can also influence feelings of attachment. (See Key 45.)

- You might experience a better personality "fit" with one twin. This is more common with fraternal twins because they usually have different temperaments. Again, increased interactions with the favored twin are typical.

Unit bonding

Unlike parents who first bond more with one twin, you might feel close to and protective of your twins as a unit before forming an attachment to each individual twin. *Unit bonding* is more likely to occur if you had access to both twins within hours of their birth.

Unit bonding tends to lead to *unit thinking*—considering twins as a single entity. One parent described this phenomenon by saying, "It seems like I have only one baby who keeps me constantly busy, though my brain knows I have two babies and I see both of them in front of me." Unit thinking might account for the desire to dress twins alike, which essentially allows twins to take on a single image.

Unit bonding is more likely to occur with identical twins. More time is needed to form separate attachments to individuals of an identical set. Quite likely this is related more to their similar body rhythms than to their physical resemblance, since few parents have difficulty telling their twins apart.

To make the attachment process even more interesting, twins often *flip-flop*, or switch personality traits, just as you think you are getting to know them. This creates confusion when trying to get to know twins as individuals. Flip-flopping is most common with identical twins and often occurs during swings in behavioral patterns. The more similar your fraternal twins' temperaments are, the more likely you are to observe personality flip-flopping. Flip-flopping is most common during the twins' first year and recurs less often as they grow.

The more twins look and act differently, the less time it takes to recognize and attach to the individuals within a twin set. Parents of opposite-sex twins are usually the first to break through unit thinking and discover each twin's uniqueness. Since opposite-sex twins are the most different in looks and temperament, this is a logical progression.

Overlap

Your attachment experience may fall more into either the preferential or unit bonding category, but overlap usually occurs. You can feel an initial closeness to one and still find yourself emphasizing the twin unit in certain circumstances. Also, as you begin to separate and work to get to know the individuals within the twin unit, you may find you focus more on one twin and then switch your focus to the other. This is another reason that the process takes more time.

In either case

Each twin deserves a special relationship with you no matter what your attachment situation. Understanding how the attachment process differs with twins can provide a basis for improving your relationship with each child.

25

PROMOTING ATTACHMENT TO TWO

Begin today to strengthen emotional bonds with your twins no matter what their age. Good relationships do not simply "happen." Participants in any long-term relationship work at it.

- Become aware of the different attachment process with twins. Step back and take an objective look at your interactions with each twin. Ask yourself if each relationship is as good as it could or should be.

- Listen to yourself, and become aware of how often you refer to your babies as "the twins," "the boys," "the girls," or "the boy and the girl." Are you falling into unit thinking? Do you refer to only one twin by name and the other by gender or as "he," "she" or even "it," all of which are indicative of preferential attachment.

- Concentrate on responding to the twin with whom you feel less close. Consciously observe his behavioral style and experiment with different ideas to involve him in your interactions. List this baby's or child's positive qualities.

- Do not waste time feeling guilty about disparate feelings of attachment. Guilt is an unproductive expenditure of mental energy. Congratulate yourself for recognizing the problem, and use your energy for more frequent interactions with the less favored twin.

- Make a concerted effort to increase skin contact with each baby through infant massage and by holding both, together or separately, as much as possible. Alternate holding twins using some type of baby carrier. This enhances contact, while giving you the advantage of two free arms. As far as your twins are concerned, sitting in a rocking chair with Mom or Dad beats any windup swing yet invented. No child is ever too old for back rubs, hugs, and kisses.

- You may depend on infant equipment more than other parents, but always evaluate its use versus abuse or overuse, which reduces parent-twin interaction.

- Take advantage of diaper changes, feedings, and bath time to grab a few moments with each twin individually. Use your imagination to "seize the moment" with older twins.

- Once eye contact is established with one, you are in fact alone with that twin even when holding both in your arms. Talk to one twin and imitate her facial expressions and vocalizations for a few minutes, alternate to focus on the second twin.

- You spent a lot of time choosing your twins' names, so use them. Go out of your way to repeat each twin's name whenever you make eye contact. Each one learns to appreciate that a name is special and a sign of uniqueness.

- Respond first to each child, not "the twins." Each twin has different needs, and these needs change over time. Whenever you fall into unit thinking, ask yourself how you would respond if these two children, who happen to be twins, were a year apart. You would not worry about equality and would give each child the kind of attention needed.

The emotional ties built during infancy set the tone for a lifelong relationship with each child. As with all relationships, they continue to require an investment of your time, energy, and commitment if these bonds are to endure and become even stronger.

26

∿∿

INDIVIDUALITY ISSUES

P arents have a fundamental role in the development of the relationship between twins. You decide what to call them, choose their clothing and toys, separate them on occasion or keep them together, and so on. Whether these decisions are made consciously or not, your approach to raising twins favors their twinship or their individuality.

Although you emphasize one aspect, you probably feel pulled toward the other from time to time. It is normal to want to treat twins as different yet the same; separate but equal. You can claim to promote your children's individuality in one breath while making certain that everyone knows you are a parent of twins in the next. Your obvious approach to twinship and individuality is rooted in the parent-twin attachment process. (Even if your twins are beyond infancy, read Keys 23, 24, and 25 if you have not already done so.)

The parent-infant relationship is considered a child's primary relationship. Not even the twin-twin relationship replaces this one. Because of the importance of the parent-child relationship, a young twin willingly caters to the parent's desire for him to act more as an individual or as half of a whole. Twins emphasize whatever helps them gain attention.

Equal but different

Many parents feel an almost fanatical desire to treat twin children equally. Dressing twins alike and devoting equal time to each relates as much to equality-mania as to unit thinking. Some parents worry that their twins or other people might think one twin is loved more if both are not treated exactly the same. Also, parenting duties are doubled with multiples, so equal treatment can contribute to an organized approach to child care.

The twins compound the problem. Just about the time you finally get to know them as two different persons, they enter the jealousy stage and demand equal treatment. If one has something, the other immediately wants it, too.

Respond to each child separately instead of responding to "the twins." You are not obligated to treat them equally and it is unrealistic to try. Twins are two separate people, like any other two people. Each has a different need for your time and attention, and the needs of both change as they grow. After all, you would not hesitate to respond differently to siblings born a year apart.

The celebrity syndrome (CS)

Our culture adores twins and considers them special. They become celebrities, commanding attention wherever they go. As their parent, you become a celebrity and gain attention simply by giving birth to more than one baby at a time. It is fun to bask in the limelight that twins bring. Face it, there are times when society's adulation may help you make it through the day. Do not feel guilty for taking advantage occasionally of your infant or toddler twins' celebrity. Think of it as a coping mechanism!

Problems arise only if your perspective disappears and you begin to take your celebrity status seriously. When this occurs you stress your children's twinship at the expense of their individuality, since your celebrity status is tied to the twins' specialness as a unit. Beware, the celebrity syndrome can strike parents no matter what the age of their twins.

Are you in danger of succumbing to the celebrity syndrome? Give yourself CS points if you:

1. Frequently refer to your children as "the twins" instead of by name—and add points if others do, too;
2. Ever boast that you have difficulty telling your twins apart—add points if said in front of your twins;
3. Inform others that your little darling has a twin when you are out with only one—add points if this is said within hearing range of the little darling, or;
4. Encourage the wearing of look-alike outfits, including look-alike outfits in different colors—add CS points for toddlers, preschoolers, and older children able to help choose their clothing and dress themselves.

A high score does not necessarily mean that you have been seduced by the celebrity syndrome, but you may want to ask yourself why you seem to be treating them as a unit. Is it for you or for them?

Resolving individuality issues

Once you truly get to know each twin, it is impossible to treat them as anything other than two individuals. Twin-related concerns, such as how to dress them or when to separate them become meaningless. Such decisions then depend on each child's current needs. They are not determined arbitrarily because of the twinship.

The temptation to enjoy your celebrity status and the desire to give twins equal time does not completely disappear as they grow. If you concentrate on your relationship with each of your twins, the word *twin* alone soon becomes a poor definition for either child. At the same time they will be developing a relationship with each other, and you will begin to see what a special part twinship plays in the development of both.

27

HOW OTHERS VIEW YOUR TWINS

Y ou set the tone for how your relatives and friends view
your twins. If you encourage others to see your twins as
individuals instead of a unit, they probably will. Others
may need a subtle nudge in the right direction, but with a little guidance you usually can secure their cooperation.

If you call your children "the twins," others will call
them "the twins." Call each of your twins by name, and ask
others to do the same. If someone forgets, restate your preference. Something like, "We prefer that you call them Mark
and Andrew since they are two separate persons," will do.
Remind the persistent resistors, but avoid long or irritated
dissertations on why this is necessary. Speeches merely reinforce your children's twinship rather than their individuality.

Parties and gifts

You may have to tell well-meaning friends and relatives
to give separate cards and gifts for birthdays and holidays.
Explain how joint gifts and cards make twins feel lumped
together. Let them know that twins usually prefer two inex-
pensive gifts unless it is something really big, easily shared or
used at the same time, and wanted by both.

As your twins age, each probably will have a separate
party or invite her own separate friends to a combined party.
It is up to you to take the initiative as to how you want these
situations handled. If you do not ask guests' parents to send a

gift only for the twin who invited their child, some will send gifts for each twin and other parents only for one. An unequal number of gifts often creates hurt feelings for the twin with fewer gifts.

You, the celebrity

You become a celebrity when your twins are born. Strangers feel free to invade your privacy, referring to your children in the third person even when your twins are with you. They presume familiarity and sometimes ask personal and embarrassing questions and have been known to make ridiculous and even insulting comments!

Forgive these offenses as part of human nature, but be prepared to handle invasions of privacy.

- You may resent positive *and* negative comments, such as "double trouble," or "double blessing," which minimize your situation by reducing this complex and intense experience to something trivial. You could respond with the opposite phrase, either positive or negative, regardless of how you feel at that moment, or you could say nothing. You do not have to allow a total stranger to have the final say.
- Expect questions about your fertility and how the twins were conceived, but do not think you have to respond with anything but a polite, "Why do you ask?" This throws the question back at the questioner.
- Some people feel that if they compliment one twin it is OK to insult the other. How do you respond when someone says, "Linda has such beautiful blue eyes. Isn't it a shame that Susan's are hazel?" Simply say, "We like hazel, too."
- You may deal with preconceived notions, such as one twin is good and one is bad.
- When you have twins, many people assume that your family is complete. This is especially true if you have girl-boy twins. What are you supposed to say when someone

approaches with the comment, "How wonderful. You got it all over with at once!"? Having more children or not is your choice, and you do not have to defend your decision. Again, answer a question with a question, for instance, "Why would you say that?" or respond with a "maybe" and a mysterious look.

- On a cheerier note, there are certain advantages to your newly found celebrity status. People often tolerate incredibly rambunctious behavior from twins when they would not tolerate such carrying on from a single child. At those times, dress twins alike and accept other's patient understanding as your due!

Teachers

Your twins will spend most of their time away from home in school, so teachers have a great influence on how twins view themselves. Teachers should follow your lead. Schedule separate conferences for each twin, and unless the discussion centers on something that concerns their twinship, do not mention the other twin. Watch for indications that faculty and staff are confusing the two. This sometimes happens even when twins are separated. One mother scheduled a conference to discuss one twin's feelings of inadequacy, only to be told that he had received numerous honors during the year. It was not until she asked for a list of these awards that teachers realized it was his twin who received every one. (See Key 43.)

Self-image

You can only control your own views and how you treat your twins. If, despite your best efforts, others continue to treat your twins as a unit, it should not have a devastating effect on either. The clearest picture they have of themselves comes from you. The strong self-image you establish during their childhoods will probably carry them through.

28

THE ADJUSTMENT PERIOD

You probably envisioned life with newborn twins while pregnant. The twins of pregnant daydreams eat and sleep on a predictable, pleasant schedule that allows for several hours of uninterrupted parental sleep at night. Daydream twins rarely cry, and if they do, they are easily comforted. The mother of your fantasy quickly recovers from the physical changes of multiple pregnancy and childbirth. Fatigue never touches her. This well-rested woman has plenty of patience as she lovingly cares for her two infants. Of course, the dream husband always pitches in to help. He knows exactly what is needed without you asking.

The idealized fantasy family with twin infants is perfect. Real families with two newborns are not. This Key focuses on what you can realistically expect during the initial adjustment period after your twins' homecoming.

Getting back to normal

Most new parents say they cannot wait to "get back to normal." They plan to fit their new babies into the predictable daily routine they had before pregnancy. The first few months of infancy are often marked more by disruption of routine rather than its restoration. Fitting two newborns into life is even more disruptive. When this disruption is unexpected, you may feel confused and frustrated with the loss of control over daily events.

Unlike a prenatal fantasy body, your real postpartum body feels tired and achy for several weeks. It has been through a lot in a short time. Your babies have been through a lot in a short time, too. Each has a unique response to life outside the womb, and you must figure out the differences in their approaches to this adaptation. Real babies have not read the child care book guidelines about infant schedules. They cannot understand that you need more, not less sleep after a multiple birth. Is it any wonder that you sometimes feel overwhelmed trying to figure out and meet the needs of two different newborns while also trying to meet important physical and emotional needs of your own and other family members? (See Keys 30 and 31.)

Rest assured, this chaotic condition is temporary. Although you can never return to your prepregnant routine, a "new normal" routine *will* develop. However, you have to compromise to discover this new normal routine, since you are more mature than your babies.

Influences on routine

Your twins' inborn behaviors and your attempts to differentiate between them affect your perception of an evolving predictable routine. You may not realize that a daily routine is developing when you are busy caring for two newborns, or you may feel more compelled to impose an organized schedule on your babies and household than a parent of a single newborn. Whether you work at developing a schedule or simply take each day as it comes, a fairly predictable daily routine generally emerges by three months.

It is very easy to compare your family with one that recently gave birth to a single new baby. That other family seems to have drawn the loose ends into a routine weeks ago and here you still sit in a state of confusion. Avoid the temptation of comparing yourself with anyone else. After all, you are trying to get to know and integrate two unique persons into your life-style.

It takes time to let go of a former routine and your prenatal fantasies. Give yourself and your twins time to find a pattern in daily life. Your new normal life with twins will exceed the expectations of your fantasies. After all, the little persons you now have are far more interesting than the children you thought you wanted in your prenatal daydreams.

29

HOUSEHOLD ORGANIZATION

I t is so exciting and time consuming parenting twins that household organization and routine seem part of a distant past. Relax and enjoy your babies and your new role as parents of twins. In a short time the house becomes organized around the needs of your newest additions. A new routine emerges that suits your family situation. This transition may come slowly and resemble your old pattern so little that you may not even recognize it for what it is.

Give yourself some time before you establish a routine. Let your babies settle into a routine of their own first, then work around it. Be flexible. During the first few months, your routine will undergo major changes as the babies mature and the family adjusts to their presence.

Prioritizing tasks is the key to any successful routine. Your newborns must be your top priority. Infants cannot and should not be put off. You cannot reason with babies. They have certain needs that must be met, and these needs do not change simply because they come to you as a pair. Any organizational system must recognize and meet the twins needs while also meeting your family's basic needs.

The key issues for most busy parents of twins are feeding babies and the rest of the family, meeting sleep needs, doing the laundry, and keeping up with the housework. "Keep it simple" should become your motto for housekeeping. By doing so, you "buy" time to spend caring for your babies.

Put the immaculate, picture-perfect house on hold for awhile. Caring for twins, even calm easygoing twins, is a tremendous time commitment. Nothing can take the place of the time you spend with your children. Take shortcuts in other parts of your life, not with your babies.

Laundry

- If you wash diapers, do not fold them. Divide them into laundry baskets as you take them out of the dryer and use them from there. Disposables or a diaper service saves even more time.
- You can throw the twins' laundry (except diapers) in with the family's wash unless either has sensitive skin.
- Forget you own an iron. Wear only wash and wear clothes that do not wrinkle if you fold or hang them immediately from the dryer.
- Let each family member put his or her clean clothes away. Even preschoolers can accomplish this if you put clothes into small baskets.
- Place flannelette pads under each baby's head and/or diaper area in their cribs. Often you need to change only these rather than an entire sheet.

Household routine

The following suggestions may also help you streamline:

- Get some household help. Your husband can offer his services, or hire someone part time or full time. (See Key 21.)
- Keep diaper-changing paraphernalia, including diaper pails, on each level of your house.
- Bathe your babies every other day or less frequently. Keeping their diaper areas and faces clean is usually enough.
- Remove knickknacks now. Be grateful that dusting them is no longer part of daily life.
- If you place a box or basket in each room to *toss* toys into, any room can appear neat with a minimum of effort. Even

toddlers can help with pick up, and *tossing* can be a good outlet for frustrations.

- Use a Crockpot and microwave. The Crockpot allows you to prepare meals at your convenience. The microwave allows last-minute preparation when father is home to watch the babies, for example.
- Use dried, frozen, and already chopped ingredients.
- Double recipes and freeze one meal to be used later.
- When ordering carryout make use of healthy soup and salad bars instead of greasy fast-food hamburgers.
- Shop by catalog. You may pay a little more for some items, but you probably save because you avoid impulse buying. No price tag can be put on the time and effort this saves.
- Consider using delivery services available in your area. Is there a grocery store that delivers? There are still milkmen out there, too, and they generally carry other dairy products. The pharmacy that delivers your prescriptions can also deliver baby formula, disposable diapers, or anything else they carry.
- Become acquainted with all the drive-through services, such as dry cleaner, bank, photo finishing, and food.
- Make use of nonessential but helpful equipment. An answering machine allows you to return calls when talking is convenient. A portable phone lets you work while you talk. A food processor can cut time in the kitchen.
- *Accept any and all offers of help.* Friends or relatives can do your grocery shopping, bring in an occasional meal, fold your laundry, vacuum, or wash dishes.

Make time in your routine for your husband and your other children. Include yourself, too. You need time to reenergize. You are as important as the other members of your family. (See Key 17.)

30

EARLY DIFFERENTIATION

Bonding, differentiation, and individualizing your twins are closely linked. Looking for differences between your newborn twins is one way you begin to know them as individuals. Whether twins are identical or fraternal influences this differentiation process.

Physical differences

No two people look exactly alike, not even identical twins. There are *always* physical differences. These will be very obvious for some sets of fraternal twins and more subtle for other fraternal twin sets and most identical sets.

You probably will have little difficulty telling your twins apart after the first few days or weeks. Frequently, one identical twin has a longer, thinner face and one a fuller face. Each often has a different look about the eyes. One sometimes has a birthmark that the other does not have. It may be more difficult to tell twins apart while they sleep because their personalities are not influencing their features.

Behavior

Temperament and its influence on behavior are, like physical features, related to heredity. Each twin's behavioral approach to situations and eventual personality is a combination of genetic temperament traits plus all the environmental factors influencing behavioral response. Newborns can no more control their behavioral style than they can their eye color or facial features.

- Just as they look alike, identical twins tend to behave alike. So if you have one calm, easygoing identical twin, both probably are easygoing, but if one leans toward fussiness, so will the other. However, their expression of temperament traits varies in degree between them or they may take turns *(flip-flop)* expressing some traits. (See Key 24.)
- Like any siblings, fraternal twins may have similar or very different behavioral styles. You may worry unnecessarily if you compare an active, fussy baby with an observant, placid twin.
- The internal biological clock governing sleep-wake cycles is also determined genetically. Identical twins are more likely to share similar sleep-wake cycles, and fraternal twins are more likely to wake at different times.

Growth and development

Your twins' developmental timetables may be similar or quite different. Identical twins tend to gain about the same amount of weight each month, grow a similar number of inches, and develop physical skills at a comparable rate. This is true for some sets of fraternal twins, but other fraternal sets vary widely within the normal range for development.

- The process of differentiation is easier and takes less time when twins' appearance, rate of development, or behavior are different.
- If fraternal twins have different patterns of growth, you may feel concern. Both may have normal growth patterns, but one simply inherited Uncle Bill's large muscular physique, and the other has Grandma's petite, wiry frame.
- Different patterns of development can also be confusing. When one pays rapt attention to a colorful mobile and the other could care less, remember there is a wide range of normal for many developmental skills.

Promoting differentiation

No matter what type of twins you have, you can enhance the differentiation process even on the busiest day.

- Look for physical differences if your twins are close in appearance. Until you are certain who is who, find a way to positively identify one. Polish a finger or toenail of one twin. You could leave a hospital identification bracelet on one twin, but take an extra one or two home to change it as that twin's wrist grows.
- You spent a lot of time choosing each twin's name. Refer to each by name whenever you make eye contact and talk to one.
- Take photographs of your twins together *and* separately.
- Do not feel concerned for now if you are compelled to dress your twins alike. Consider dressing them in look-alike outfits in different colors or in different outfits of the same color. This strategy recognizes both their twinship and their separateness.
- Become familiar with the range of normal variation in infant growth and development. Chart premature twins' development from their due date for full term rather than their actual birth date. Read about growth and development for each age group before your twins reach it. Also, refer to this reference book whenever one masters a skill before the other. (See Appendix A for Suggested Reading.)
- Look for each infant's strengths, and nurture them. If one or both twins has a more difficult temperament, remember that babies cannot be "good" or "bad." Every challenging quality has positive aspects. Often challenging babies are very sensitive and bright persons. (See Key 31.)
- Ignore people who say you should never compare your twins. This advice is not realistic. Discovering twins' differences naturally leads to making comparisons between

them. This is not a problem, as long as you make the distinction between comparison and labeling. *Comparisons* are general and flexible and change as your children grow and change. *Labels*, such as the happy twin, the smart twin, or the moody twin, are rigid and may stick even when they no longer apply.

• Note your twins' similarities as well as their differences. This is a part of differentiation as well.

You can influence each twin's inborn pattern of development, but you cannot change it completely. If you provide a stimulating environment for both twins, introduce each to a variety of experiences, and remember that you are the most important toy either will ever have, you allow them to achieve their individual potentials—whatever that is for either twin.

Early differentiation—noticing and comparing twins' differences and similarities—provides a "black and white" view of the members within a twin set. It is the foundation for recognizing each twin as a unique individual and for the eventual disposal of unit thinking. (See Keys 24, 25, and 26.)

31

COPING WITH CRYING

C rying is an important form of infant communication, but translating the cries of two babies can be over-whelming at times. You may feel there is not enough of you to go around when both twins cry at once. When twins take turns crying, it may seem that a baby is crying every minute of the day. There are many ways to cope with double crying. What works for one baby may not work for the other.

Why twins cry

Your twins' fussiness or colic is probably not the result of something you are doing wrong. Crying usually has more to do with each baby's temperament than with anything you do or do not do. It is more likely that their crying makes you feel tense than that your tension makes them cry.

Handling overstimulated babies sometimes increases crying. Lay a crying baby in a crib in a quiet room. It will become obvious within 5 to 15 minutes if the baby is settling. If the baby is still crying after that time, try another interven-tion. *Do not let a baby continue to cry unattended.*

Things in the environment occasionally contribute to fussiness. Either might be sensitive to something passing through breast milk or to an ingredient in the formula. Infant fluoride or iron upsets some babies. *(Always check with their medical professional before changing their diets in any way.)* They might be irritated by secondhand cigarette smoke, household sprays, or powders.

How to handle trying, crying times

Positive reminders of your good fortune can help you get through the trying, crying times. While out strolling, enjoy all the pats on the back you receive for the amazing feat of giving birth to and caring for twins. Relish the praise heaped upon your adorable babies. Of course, this may not always work, so you might find these suggestions helpful:

- If you can predict fussy times, have help available to get through those hours when both twins need comforting.

- Use helpful equipment. Carefully prop newborns in infant swings using rolled blankets or diapers. Let an infant's own motion rock her in a bouncer seat. Experiment with different pacifiers. Test drive your new double stroller to soothe babies in the fresh air.

- "White noise," a rhythmic, staticky sound like that made by motors or a radio not tuned to a station calms some babies. Others are soothed by listening to the familiar sounds of the womb. Some infant equipment shops sell tapes of uterine sounds or a device that produces a quiet white noise.

If your fretful babies respond best to body contact with you:

- Get a comfortable rocking chair that accommodates you and both babies. Rocking will calm all three of you! Keep a portable lawn chair rocker in your car in case you visit rockerless relatives or friends.

- Infant carriers allow you to keep twins close, yet you still have a free hand or two.

    1. Double carriers are available.
    2. Some parents use two single carriers together, "wearing" one baby in front and one in back, or both crisscrossed in front.
    3. Your ability to simultaneously carry twins depends on your twins' weights and activity levels.

4. Often only one baby needs to ride in the carrier or sling at any one time.

- It is not safe to briefly carry a twin in each arm, since you have no way to break a fall. Always be aware of the potential dangers of carrying both. *Do not allow helpers to carry both.*

Your feelings

It is all right to feel ambivalent about having twins when one or both are particularly fussy babies. Obviously, it is easier to care for two even-tempered babies than two babies who are fussy or have colic. Ambivalent feelings do not mean you would give either twin back if you could!

- You can have one easygoing twin and one who demands a lot of attention. If both are fussy, one usually cries more. You may feel torn when one needs more of your time than the other. Do not worry about responding to the individual needs of each twin.

  The more quiet twin usually "asks" for attention when it is needed. You might feel better if you spend some time alone with the less demanding twin to avoid the potential for benign neglect.

- You may feel resentful at times if one or both twins is fussy or difficult to comfort. That is OK. Life *would* be more pleasant without all of this crying. Although resentment may be aimed at the fussier twin initially, you may feel closer sooner to the baby who demands more interaction.

- It is natural to have negative feelings, as long as you do not take your feelings out on the twins. Your crying babies feel as frustrated as you do. They would tell you what they need if they could.

- Exercise, meditate, or scream into a pillow to release pent up frustration. Cry along with your twins—it is as great a tension reliever for you as for your babies!

- You eventually learn to differentiate each baby's various cries and to distinguish one twin's cries from the other, although some babies are always more difficult to "read."
- See Barron's *Keys to Calming the Fussy Baby* for additional suggestions.

Although coping with crying can be one of the most distressing aspects of caring for newborn twins, take heart! Fussy times and colic are usually a memory by three to five months. Until then, hang on to the double lifesavers of flexibility and a sense of humor.

32

SLEEP

Sleep is a major concern for new parents of twins. Strategies that work for a family with one infant are often inappropriate for families with twins. Some twins sleep through the night almost immediately but most do not. It helps to be prepared to cope with this aspect of parenting two.

Fatigue related to your twin pregnancy and delivery has an impact on your own need for sleep. If you had a cesarean delivery, you are recovering from major surgery as well as childbirth. You are pushing your body beyond its normal limits if you do not rest.

Unfortunately, your sleep needs and your twins' needs rarely coincide. Newborns cannot sleep for long periods without being fed. Sleeping four to five hours is sleeping through the night, but many babies do not have a sleep stretch even this long. Most premies must be awakened and fed more often than this.

Remember

Be realistic in your expectations for yourself, your babies' father, and your twins. Your babies need time to adjust to their new environment before you worry about their sleep patterns.

- Twins seldom disturb each other when they share a crib, and many sleep better.
- Keep a sleep chart for each baby to help you recognize their individual patterns. You can see with the help of a

chart if your twins are each getting a normal amount of sleep.

• Proponents of sleep training do not suggest trying it before five to seven months. With premature twins, count months from the due date, not the birth date.

Try

Your ability to manipulate both infants' sleep-wake cycles depends on each baby's temperament and inherent body rhythms. One twin may be able to go along with whatever changes you make, but the other resists every attempt to replace her natural cycle with an artificial routine. If you want to modify either twin's routine, give anything you try a chance to work. It may take several days before you notice some change.

Juggle sleeping arrangements until you find one that works best for the family while meeting your babies' needs. What works today may not work tomorrow. Be prepared to change, and be flexible.

If your babies are being bottlefed:

1. Alternate "night duty." One parent handles all infant care for both babies while the other parent sleeps through the night.
2. One of you can take the late evening feeding while the other goes to bed early and takes the middle of the night or early morning feedings. This usually gives each parent a four to six hour stretch of sleep.

Father cannot breastfeed twins, but he certainly can get out of bed, change the babies, bring them to mother to nurse, soothe a waiting baby, and return them to their cribs.

Distinguish nighttime from daytime. Keep the room dark and quiet, and stimulate the babies as little as possible during feedings. Do not turn on the TV or radio.

Most parents prefer that their twins be on similar schedules. To accomplish this, try waking the second twin with the first twin or soon after the first awakens. You can even wake one twin before the other if one has a predictable waking time.

The complaint of having "days and nights mixed up" is double trouble for the parents of twins. Try waking them more frequently during the day to see if they lengthen their nighttime sleep periods. The family bed has saved many a night's sleep for some parents.

Parents who bring their twins to bed with them, even for part of the night, say the babies seem to wake less often and need less comforting. (See Appendix A for books on the family bed.)

The purpose of sleep training is to help your older infant twins learn to soothe themselves to sleep. It does not mean letting them "cry it out." If they can go long periods without needing to feed, give them water instead of formula when they wake and/or rub their backs instead of picking them up. (See Appendix A for books on sleep training.)

Parents' sleep

Evaluate your own sleep needs. You are not doing justice to yourself or your twins if you become a "walking zombie" because you are overtired. Try to sleep when you sleep best, taking your own body rhythms into account.

- After the first hectic months, attempt to set an early bedtime for your twins. You will have time to wind down before you go to sleep.
- Nap or rest during the day when your babies nap.
- Ask a friend or hire someone to babysit for a couple of hours while you sleep. Nap out of hearing range or have the

care giver take your twins for a walk. You may not sleep if you hear your babies fussing.

- Review your twins' sleep charts. You may discover a pattern that enables you to reorganize your routine to get more sleep.
- If you are a morning person, go to bed an hour earlier than usual.
- If you are a night person, occasionally arrange for someone else to get your twins up in the morning. Weekends provide the perfect opportunity for Dad to enjoy his twins while Mom sleeps.

Night waking does not bother your babies, it bothers you. Infants who have difficulty sleeping through the night or adjusting to change are not trying to be manipulative or thwart you. They simply are listening to their bodies just as you must listen to yours. As adults, both parents must readjust until each family member's sleep cycle is in sync with the others.

33

GETTING OUT

Both you and your twins need the stimulation of a different environment. A long walk gives you exercise and your babies fresh air. A trip to a shopping mall or out for lunch, even if you are alone with your babies, provides you with an adult environment and frequently a chance for conversation, too. Most parents of twins are stopped repeatedly by curious strangers asking questions and making positive comments about "the twins." Visits to friends and relatives leave many parents and babies feeling renewed and refreshed.

Getting out with two babies requires organization, but with planning you can accomplish the task with a minimum amount of effort. *Always* buckle each baby into an approved car seat even if traveling only a short distance.

The diaper bag

Keep your diaper bag stocked with essentials—extra diapers, bottles, clothing, plastic bags for soiled diapers, a stain remover stick to use on soiled clothing, wipes to clean hands and diaper areas, pacifiers, and a portable changing pad. Restock your bag after your return home, so you do not have to pack as you are going out the door. Then you will not worry that you have forgotten something critical.

Use a large diaper bag that can be slung over your shoulder. You need your hands and arms free for babies. Many mothers use a backpack instead of a conventional diaper bag.

Place your purse, or essential items, into your diaper bag or a fanny pack so you have one less thing to carry.

The stroller

Your twin stroller is *the* essential piece of equipment because it is your lifeline to the outside world. It empowers and puts you in control. It provides you with the means and flexibility to leave home with your twins without having to ask another adult to help.

These suggestions for use of a stroller may help you streamline outings:

- Store the twins' stroller in your car. That means one less trip to the car when leaving the house.
- Never leave home without the stroller even if you don't think you'll use it. If you have car trouble you may need to remove the babies from the car, and how would you manage that without the stroller?
- If you do not want to attract attention, use a carrier for one baby and a single stroller for the other. By the time most people realize you have twins, you will have passed them. (Rotate the twin in the stroller and the twin who is carried.)

The grocery

Everyone needs food, so the grocery store is frequently the first place a parent of twins will venture with two babies in tow. You should follow certain guidelines because the distractions inherent in this outing may lead to being inattentive to your babies. The following hints can be applied to any store where shopping carts are used.

Two carts: Infant seats and car seats often fit into the seat portion of large carts. Buckle one baby into the seat portion of the cart. (Baby should be buckled into the car seat; the car seat should be strapped into the cart.) Place the other baby in the car seat in the basket of the cart. Place groceries in a second cart that you pull behind. Always keep the babies in the front cart so you can see them.

When your babies can sit, strap or harness each one into a separate cart and divide your groceries between them, pulling the heavier and pushing the lighter.

One cart: Place the second baby in a carrier or backpack. Do not carry the second twin while pushing the cart. You need two hands to handle the other baby if she should need you.

Safety and the grocery

Use caution with shopping carts. Small carts are not as stable as large carts. The seats sometimes flip, causing children to strike their heads on the bottom of the cart.

When your twins begin to climb you will need harnesses to keep them seated. The straps provided with the carts do not provide sufficient safety.

Once your twins can sit, it may seem logical to place one baby in the seat and the other in the body of a shopping cart. This is *never* safe. Carts are designed and balanced to hold nonmovable objects. Even a young child can shift the weight in the body of a cart enough to overturn it.

Only one

There will be times when you may want to take only one baby with you or you may feel uncomfortable taking two. One mother of twins always took one baby to church with her on Sunday because it provided her with a whole hour to cuddle one twin. This kind of outing is a treat for both you and the baby. You are able to focus calmly on one twin, and that twin gets your undivided attention. Plan your one-on-one excursion during a calm period or naptime for the one left home so he is not upset while you are gone.

People generally crave socialization and mobility. It may be more of a challenge to venture forth with twins, but the psychological and emotional rewards for both parents and twins makes the effort well worth the trouble.

34

INFANCY: THREE TO SIX MONTHS

A routine has finally emerged after the unpredictability of the newborn period. You may not realize it, but you are probably becoming a master of organization and efficiency as you care for two babies, race through household chores, and perhaps even schedule a moment for yourself. It may still be hectic, but you have a glimpse of the "new normal" life after twins. This Key describes the changes to expect during your twins' second three months.

Life with twins

Your twins are now social beings. Both eagerly interact with you. Each begins to recognize that you are someone very special.

- There is nothing to compare with two small, smiling faces and four waving arms and legs greeting your arrival. Could your twins find a better way to reward you for all the time and attention you give them?
- Few twins interact much with one another at this age. One twin may initiate physical contact with the other, such as touching hands if you lay them side by side, and some occasionally make eye contact.
- You may love your twins' smiles, but do not expect an equal number from both. Do not take it personally if one is stingier with smiles, and do not equate that twin's soberness with unhappiness.

- You probably feel more in tune with each twin's behavioral style and have a good idea which soothing techniques work for each. The subtleties of each twin's personality may escape you as differentiation continues. (See Key 30.)
- Colic and fussy spells generally disappear or diminish during these months, and usually both twins are easier to comfort. Both may be irritable at times, though, particularly when overtired. Your "high need" or supersensitive twin demands more attention, but continue to respond to each baby instead of to "the twins."
- By now your premature or very small newborns have begun to look more like "regular" babies and you probably feel more comfortable handling them.

Growth and development

Studies indicate that compared with a single infant, twins tend to receive less physical and verbal stimulation from parents. Immersed in infant care tasks, some parents apparently talk to and play with twins less, yet it is this kind of stimulation that promotes skill development. Encouraging development does not take much extra time if you incorporate it into your care-giving tasks, but you must make a point to do it.

Be alert for, applaud, and encourage each twin's efforts to reach every new milestone, whether it is one twin's interest in a rattle or the other's attempts to roll over.

You are the most interesting toy either has.

1. Seize a minute to interact with one twin alone whether changing a diaper, wiping a face, or simply sharing a quiet moment alone. Minutes add up. Do not lose opportunities for lots of hugs, kisses, and chances to reinforce each twin's name as you say, "I love you, Michael!"

2. Lay twins next to one another on a pad on the floor. Kneel at their feet, and alternate making eye contact and playing with each. This is a great way to accomplish doubled diaper-changing duty.

3. Mimic the faces and sounds each makes, and be sure that twin can see you do it.

4. Talk to each twin as you care for them. As you work around the house, describe and explain things. Ask them questions, although they cannot respond.

5. You sometimes need the extra "arms" of bouncer chairs or windup swings, but you remain the superior infant carrier. The stimulation twins receive in your arms and on your lap is irreplaceable.

Most developmental toys can be made easily from items available in your home.

Check both twins' progress in your growth and development book. Consult the doctor if you have a question or are concerned about either. (See Key 30.)

Continue to chart premature twins' development from their due date rather than from their actual birth date.

Daily routine

Most babies have established a fairly predictable daily routine by three months. Your twins' routines may not be exactly what you consider ideal.

Both twins are awake longer. Identical twins are more likely to take their one to three daily naps at the same times; fraternal twins' napping patterns may be more dissimilar.

You can probably estimate each twin's naptime, bedtime, and nighttime feedings. Although either or both may sleep for longer periods at night, the need of either twin for night feedings often continues. (See Key 32.)

If you have been waking one twin with or after the other for night feedings, see what happens if you let that second twin sleep. You can miss the readiness of one to sleep longer or through the night by continuing to wake both.

Your twins may drop one or two feedings whether breast or bottlefed—with luck this will be a night feeding! Those still preferring frequent feedings usually have become extremely efficient, so feedings take less time. Your twins interact with you during feedings now, so continue to hold them. Each begins to be easily distracted by the other during feedings.

One or both twins may become interested in solid food before six months. Never give anything to babies other than breast milk or formula before discussing it with the doctor. (To coordinate solid feedings, see Key 35.)

Three to six months is often a period of relative calm after a wild storm. Appreciate it. Review how far you have come, and give yourself a well-deserved pat on the back!

35

~~~~~~

INFANCY: SIX TO NINE MONTHS

This is a period of transition for your twins. Their once all-liquid diet begins to include solid foods. Many move from your lap to the floor as their mobility increases and they begin to explore the frontiers of home. Keeping up with these changes for two babies can be an exciting challenge.

Growth and development

Differences related to twin type may seem more obvious as twins evolve into older babies. Each one's appearance, behavioral style, and activity level become more sharply defined.

Fraternal twins' approaches to developmental skills can be extremely varied, particularly for girl-boy twins. One twin may focus more on large motor activity while the other concentrates on developing fine motor control. Often each employs a completely different method for developing the same skill.

Identical twins often work on developing the same skills at the same time and/or in exactly the same way even when neither can see the other.

Whether either or both is more the "physical" or the "observer" type, babies this age are compelled to physically experience objects with their hands and mouths. (See Key 37.)

There is nothing wrong with the intermittent use of equipment, such as play yards and walkers. Do not *overuse* such equipment, which is a greater temptation when keeping track of two babies. It is vital for the proper development of each twin's body and brain that both have many daily opportunities to begin exploring your home while moving about on their own arms and legs. You, and everything in your home, are your twins' most important developmental toys.

Continue to talk to each twin separately. Establish eye contact when a twin makes sounds, and mimic that twin's sounds. Comparing the sounds each twin makes can bolster differentiation. (See Keys 31 and 35.)

• Some babies are irritable while teething, and others never seem bothered. Fraternal twins' reactions are usually more varied. Often each new tooth appears in both identical twins' mouths within days or even hours of one another, but one fraternal twin can have several teeth before the other gets any.
• Your twins are probably catching more minor illnesses. Whatever one twin contracts, the other usually comes down with as well. The first twin with a contagious disease generally exposes the other to it before the first displays any symptoms. It is virtually impossible to prevent this, although special precautions may be worth the effort if one twin already has a compromising health condition.

Continue charting premature twins' development according to the due date. Consult a growth and development book when you have questions or concerns about either twin.

Starting solids
This is an exciting step in development, but do not rush it. It only makes life with twins more enjoyable if they are ready for solid foods.

- Each twin may signal readiness in different ways.
- Identical twins are more likely to be ready and interested in solids at about the same time. Fraternal twins' readiness or interest can vary by several weeks or even months.
- When spoon-feeding twins simultaneously, place them side by side in two infant seats, two high chairs, or a double stroller. Use the same bowl and spoon with both. Alternate giving a bite to one twin and then the other.
- Each may wait more patiently for a bite of solids if you give both a spoon to hold while you feed them.
- Each parent can feed solids to one twin for at least one meal a day. Alternate twins and parents, so both parents gain individual time with each twin. If you feed twins before you eat, they may sit still in their high chairs while the rest of the family eats.
- Your twins still need the security of your arms for some feedings. They may pat your breasts, want to hold their bottles, or hold each other's hand as you hold them for feedings.
- Making baby food or switching to cow's milk may seem like good ways to cut costs when buying food for two babies, yet neither is safe under certain circumstances. Discuss all aspects of introducing solid foods with the doctor.

Routine

A daily routine continues to evolve as babies spend more time occupying themselves with motor skill development.

- One or both twins may drop a nap.
- Expect a drop in the number of breast or bottlefeedings for either as their individual interest in solid food increases.
- Daily baths often become a necessity as twins spend more time on the floor or discover creative uses for solid food. Most twins enjoy bathing together once they can sit unsupported. This also saves time and energy. (See Key 37.)

• Whether as a result of teething or the increase in illnesses, or for other reasons, it is not unusual for one or both twins to awaken again or more often during the night. (See Key 32.)

This is an exciting time. As twins become more preoccupied with their environment, you have more time to appreciate the differences and similarities of their individual styles. You also have more time for yourself and other family members.

36

INFANCY: NINE TO
FIFTEEN MONTHS

Twins enter this stage on all fours, but they walk or run through its exit. It can be a challenge to stay one step ahead of twins at this age. When they give you a moment to slow down, you will be captivated with their blossoming twin-twin relationship. This Key gives you a glimpse of a fascinating period for twin development and suggestions for smoothing your pathway through it. (See Key 37.)

Growth and development

Twins at this stage are quite busy refining old skills and learning new ones. Each twin's personality truly unfolds, and they usually begin to spend much more time physically and/or visually interacting with one another. Twin type-related differences come more into focus.

Identical twins often have compensated for any great physical differences present at birth. Typically, their growth patterns, weights, heights, patterns of hair growth as well as color and texture, and skin tones are very close. Your identical twins still look different to you, although you may find yourself doing an occasional double take to identify one or the other.

As with other aspects of their behavioral styles, identical twins tend to be closer in motor development and activity levels. Both usually lean toward being more "physical," or both are more the "observer" type; both work harder at developing gross motor skills, or both are more involved with fine motor control.

Fraternal twins' motor development and/or activity levels may be similar or at opposite ends for normal variation in development. The boy of opposite-sex twins is more likely to have a higher level of activity and be more gross-motor oriented.

By the end of this stage, each twin should be able to understand several dozen words and respond to simple requests. If either twin has difficulty understanding, discuss it with the doctor.

There is wider variation for the development of actual speech. Generally, girls are verbal earlier than boys, and this can lead to unnecessary concern if you have opposite-sex twins. Encourage speech development by properly repeating any words either says and pointing out any object either names.

Each twin should recognize her own name and image in a mirror. If one or both does not, emphasize these while playing.

Twins sometimes seem less affected by separation anxiety than a single child as long as they remain together. You are one "home base" of security, but each twin develops a second "home base" in the other.

Either or both twins might resist going out with you separately because of their increasing involvement with the other. Neither yet understands the concept of taking turns.

The realization that you have formed an individual relationship with each twin might strike you during this period. This seems to happen earlier if you have boy-girl twins and later if twins are identical. (See Keys 24, 28, and 30.)

Feeding

Your twins' diets begin to look more "grown up." Each twin may signal readiness for new feeding skills in different ways.

Self-feeding by each twin is easiest in the long run. Initially you may need to combine spoon and self-feeding. Present each twin with a bowl containing a small amount of food and a spoon. Introduce finger foods as soon as possible.

Twins show each other interesting uses for foods, but think of it as part of development!

The combination of two babies, high activity levels, and finger foods can result in food fights. Remove each perpetrator's food and explain why. Return the food after a minute or two. Repeat this process whenever a food fight recurs. Moving their high chairs farther apart may help maintain order.

Let them drink liquids from a small cup with handles or one their hands can encircle. Cups that have lids with spouts may be more manageable and less messy.

Place a drop cloth under the high chairs for easy clean ups.

Many twins wean during this period although it is not unusual for either to continue nursing or to take a bottle. Identical twins often wean at about the same time; fraternal twins may wean months apart. Also, one twin might seem ready to wean but refuse to do so as long as the other continues breast or bottlefeeding.

Twins' physical growth and appetites slow during this stage, but their nutritional needs can differ. Even identical twins growing at the same rate may eat different amounts and kinds of foods. Each may eat more at a particular meal, but this meal might be different for each.

First birthday

Hooray! You made it. This birthday is more of a celebration for you than for the one-year-old twins, who do not understand the significance of birthdays—yet! Your twins will not care whether the neighborhood is present or if you alone commemorate their special day with them. Party plans should coincide with your needs and the time you are willing or able to spend preparing for guests.

Birthdays provide the perfect opportunity to reaffirm each twin's individuality, although as a pair they obviously share this special day. Remind guests who might bear gifts that twins are two separate persons, not a collective entity. Bake or buy (or beg from Grandma) two small cakes or cupcakes, or divide a sheet cake into two sections and decorate one for each twin. Sing "Happy Birthday" first to one twin and then the other, and alternate who is sung to first by even- and odd-numbered birthdays. Or sing to your twins once, but refer to each by name rather than "Happy Birthday dear twins."

Ready or not!

Twins can be entertaining and exasperating whirlwinds of activity at this age. Their newfound preoccupation with one another can have both pleasant and perilous consequences. Do not sit back just yet; toddler twins are even busier and more interesting!

37

~~~~~~

TWINPROOFING
THEIR WORLD

C reating a safe environment demands extra parental thought and action when two babies are distracting you. You have to be more aware of potential dangers than other parents. You must fine-tune your skills of observation and anticipation.

Every age

Certain safety adages apply for twins of all ages.

- Often one twin is injured when a parent is preoccupied with the other.
- Situations that are hazardous with one baby often are exaggerated for two.
- It is easy to underestimate either twin's physical or mental capabilities when dealing with twins' different developmental timetables.
- The more physically active each twin is, the more challenging and crucial twinproofing becomes.
- Whether because of sex-related differences or socialization, boys are more likely to engage in risk-taking behaviors resulting in injuries.
- They may take twice as long to buckle and unbuckle, but *never* start the car until both twins are properly restrained in car seats (or seat belts if older).

Most of the suggestions that follow apply double as your twins grow!

Newborn to six months

Unsafe equipment, misuse of equipment, and falls are most often responsible for accidents during the first half year.

- Do not borrow or buy used equipment, such as cribs and car seats, unless you are *certain* that it meets safety guidelines.
- *Never* lay either twin on or in anything above floor level unless you are next to *and* paying attention to that baby or the side rails are locked in place. The baby lying quietly today may roll off the changing table or sofa tomorrow. The twin in an infant seat up on a table may bounce until the seat falls off or pitch forward out of it.
- Lower crib mattresses once twins begin to roll over.
- Get down on all fours and twinproof your home for the next stage.

Six to nine months

Curiosity is crucial, but budding explorers require additional safeguarding.

Twins *quickly* find any neglected hazard. Move breakable curios and all cleaning agents and plants beyond twins' reach. Cap electrical outlets and move electrical cords now. Scan the floor frequently for small, "edible" items.

Never leave either twin unsupervised—even briefly—when their movements are confined by equipment, such as play yards or walkers. Walkers especially are associated with a large number of emergency room visits each year.

Never leave one or both twins unattended in the tub. While distracted with one twin or getting postbath clothing, one could turn on the hot water, slip and fall, or drown in as little as 1 inch of water.

Nine to fifteen months

As twins move on two feet and become more interested in one another, new safety challenges arise.

- Use safety gates to keep twins *in* or *out* of an area. Gate the top and bottom of stairways, but leave a couple of bottom steps open so they can practice climbing.
- Keep the door to the cellar locked. Basement stairways are often open and uncarpeted, which make them even more dangerous.
- If twins are allowed in the kitchen, use safety latches on all drawers and cabinets except for one "play" drawer. *Never* leave either twin in the kitchen without adult supervision. Use gates to keep them out when you are not there.
- Bathrooms should be off-limits. A toilet draws twins like a magnet. Not only do they put things into it, either could also drown in it.
- Use chest harnesses for climbers who want out of the stroller, high chairs, and shopping cart. It is more difficult to get out of a harness that fastens in the back, even with a twin's help. Harnesses with side straps and a leash option are more adaptable.
- Hard-soled, heavy, high-top shoes are generally an unnecessary expense and they can become weapons when kicking or hitting at one's twin. Flexible, soft-soled gym shoes are safer, and they support and protect early walkers' feet just as well or better.

Special hazards

Certain situations are more hazardous because parents may not realize the additional potential for injuries.

- Older siblings often leave doors ajar and forget "appetizing" collections in twins' exploration territory.
- Baby-sitters cannot appreciate the exaggerated effect of

twin distractions. Consider hiring two and assigning one to a specific twin.

- Visitors' purses often contain medications, matches, and other dangerous items.
- Pools are special attractions. They cannot be twinproofed even if covered.
- Toddler and preschool twins face additional dangers. (See Keys 39 and 42.)

Your twins' environment is wherever they happen to be. If you leave your twinproofed home, twinproof the new environment. Do not let anyone scoff at or undermine your efforts. Be alert to medications in older persons' homes.

Accidents

Despite your best efforts, one or both twins might sustain an injury. Be prepared for any possibility.

- Take infant and child cardiopulmonary resuscitation (CPR) and first-aid classes.
- Post the number for the poison control center and emergency help near every phone.
- Have syrup of ipecac available, but talk to someone at the poison control center before using it. Inducing vomiting sometimes causes additional damage.
- Go over safety instructions with anyone who provides care for one or both twins.

Every twin has the same need as any baby to explore the environment. This creates a greater challenge for you, who must keep track of two. There is no substitute for a twinproofed environment if you wish to avoid a situation that ends with "If only I had…"

38

MOVING INTO
TODDLERHOOD:
15 TO 36 MONTHS

There is nothing quite like rediscovering the world through a toddler's eyes. Of course, you have twice as much to discover, a situation that may sometimes leave you breathless. Toddler twins create a unique parenting experience because of their own developing relationship.

Socialization

Single-born toddlers mainly engage in "parallel" play: they play alongside each other but do not interact much. Twin toddlers interact a great deal, but their style usually is usually primitive. For this reason toddler twins seem to be either "kissing or killing" each other during most of their interactions. This is enhanced or minimized depending on their individual activity levels and motor orientation.

- Toddler twins learn to share much earlier than other children. Of course, they may end up fighting over the item being shared!
- Toddler twins watch out for one another. Often one twin makes certain that the other has any treat before enjoying her own. Also, they may fight with each other, but anyone who bothers either twin will have the other to contend with.
- If you punish one twin for hurting the other, the "victim" is often more upset than the "aggressor" being punished.

- Envy, an emotion not thought to emerge until the preschool years, may be seen much earlier with twins. Both often want the same thing at the same time, even if two of the same item are available.
- Jealousy and envy may give rise to competition between twins. Toddler twins compete for toys, activities, and, perhaps most of all, for **you**. This can lead to individual demands for equal time and attention from you.

Language development

Besides typical language development, you may have twin-specific language concerns.

Studies indicate that speech delays are slightly more common with twins. Prematurity and less parental stimulation are considered contributing factors. Also, both twins hear the mispronunciations of the other. Applaud each twin's efforts to speak, ask them questions that encourage them to talk, and reinforce or properly repeat whatever each says.

A twin who is more verbal or extroverted may assume the role of spokesperson for the set. Watch for this, and do not let it happen. Both twins must practice speech, and both need to learn how to make their needs known. When one answers for the other, you might say, "Thank you (spokesperson's name), but I was asking (quiet twin's name) about this." Then make eye contact with the quiet twin and restate the question.

Idioglossia is the name for the development of a special language by twins. Although many twins make up words they share for certain items or activities, few sets create a complete language. Those who do often have been left to entertain each other with little interaction with and stimulation by their parents.

You and your twins

It should be much easier to think in terms of the individuals within the twin set by now. You probably feel in tune with both the sharp contrasts and the subtleties of each personality, yet their twinship still impacts on your parenting.

Letting each twin make choices enhances individuality. (See Key 40.)

Dressing two individuals alike no longer may feel "right," yet you might find yourself compelled to continue. If you pick out several mix-and-match clothing items, you can let each twin choose what to wear each day.

Each twin is incomparable. Differentiation has ended. The comparisons you made to distinguish between your twins should end as well. Comparisons too easily lead to labeling, especially if one twin is easier to manage than the other. Little twins have big ears. They understand comparative remarks they overhear.

Each twin should have exclusive ownership of some clothing items and toys. You can initial duplicates, but they quickly learn to identify their own belongings. Toddler twins often want duplicate items to be *exactly* alike. You may spend hours finding two tricycles in different colors or two of the same doll in different outfits only to have both twins fight over the same one!

Finding a moment to spend with only one twin may be difficult. As long as both are awake, neither may let the other alone with you.

Many twins still resist even brief separations. Toddlers cannot yet understand the concept of taking turns to go out with you.

If you worry about whether one twin is dominant and one passive, remember that there are different kinds of dominance. One may be physically dominant and the other mentally dominant. Twins often flip-flop dominance. Anyway, what is wrong with being passive?

Flip-flopping usually occurs less frequently but may last longer than in the twins' first year. (See Key 24.)

When toddler twins are on the same wavelength, a third personality may emerge from their combined energy, the "twin" personality. You may discover you have each individual twin plus a joint twin personality.

Your twins' relationship

Your twins invest a lot of energy in their developing twin-twin relationship from this point on. Their interactions are the basis for this relationship, and they are forming it as they cooperate, compete, share, and fight. You need not, nor will you, always agree with their methods. They have a right to their own relationship, and they must work on it themselves. You cannot do this for them.

39

COMBINED ENERGY

Your twins are off and running, but not all twins move at the same speed. Whether your twins "walk" or "race" through toddlerhood depends on each one's activity level and motor orientation and how one twin's levels combine with those of the other. The combination of their individual levels will influence your feelings about this stage.

"Walkers" tend to be observers who prefer to let you bring the world to them. "Joggers" move at a faster pace and explore whatever is available within arms' reach. "Racers" move constantly and go up, over, around, and through for the sheer thrill or to reach any object worth their consideration.

A twin with a higher activity level often influences another at a slightly lower level to move faster, and together their pace is faster still. Frequently a racer speeds the pace of a jogger until the jogger also becomes a racer. A jogger might affect a walker, although a racer probably will not. The walker's activity level and interests may be too different to be swayed by the racer.

Identical twins are more likely than fraternal twins to have similar activity levels, and opposite-sex fraternal twins tend to be the most diverse.

Significance of pace

The higher your twins' combined level of activity, the more challenging it becomes to stay one step ahead of them.

You may wonder if your racers or racer-jogger combination are hyperactive. However, either active twin may be quite manageable and pleasant by himself. It is their combined energy that makes them more difficult to watch.

If you have two walkers, you may not understand the need for dramatic twinproofing. Beware of complacency, however. Any toddler can find herself in potentially dangerous situations even when both twins rarely seek them out.

Twin toddlerproofing

You will find that "two heads *are* better than one" when your twins dream up schemes that few single toddlers could imagine, much less implement alone. There is *nothing* that determined twin racers, and even joggers, cannot and will not get into while working in tandem. Together they can drag a chair to get something out of reach, and if each takes a drawer pull, they can see what is inside or use the drawers as steps to climb to the top of the bureau. Any new "trick" one learns is quickly taught to the other. Once learned, any trick can be used by either when apart from the twin. Incorporate the suggestions in Key 37 with these additional suggestions for active toddler twins.

- Things moved earlier should be placed even higher or stored.
- Kitchen appliances pose special problems. Parents of twins have capped stove knobs, used bungee cords to keep oven and refrigerator doors closed, and even padlocked the refrigerator.
- Lock knives, scissors, matches, and other unsafe items in a chest. Use a second locked chest for all medications and vitamins.
- Move or store furniture that poses a hazard, including pieces either twin climbs on or items with sharp edges or corners. Try removing lightweight "climbing" chairs. Use folding chairs during meals and then store them on top of the table.

- Once either twin tries to climb out of a crib, let them sleep on a mattress on the floor or place mesh domes over their cribs. They should be able to stand. (A dome should not be used if it upsets either twin.)
- If necessary, strip the bedroom of furniture, window treatments, and wall hangings. (They probably will start this for you!) Gate or use a half-door for the bedroom. Twins may stack pillows to climb over gates. Some parents separate twins in different bedrooms, but this is not always feasible.
- Check how far all your windows open, whether they lock well, and how secure the screens are. Do not place twins' beds under windows.
- Apply *slide locks* to bedroom and bathroom doors but at a level that older siblings can reach. Hook-and-eye locks are less effective, as agile twins quickly figure them out.
- Securely block balconies or outside decks that twins could go over or through.
- Twinproof your garage and yard. Tools and poisonous materials should be locked away.
- If fencing a grassy area, be sure materials used and fence height are adequate. Do not install a gate, so twins' only access to unfenced areas is through the house.
- Many twins run in different directions if not confined by a fence, their stroller, or a harness with leash. This also applies when in the car, so *insist* they stay in car seats to minimize distractions for the driver.

Energy-diverting play

Providing "twinproof" toys can help redirect your twins' energy. Consider the following when buying toys:

- *Any* toy or its pieces can become an unintentional weapon for hitting or throwing at the other twin. Check hand-size toys for weight and sharp edges or points.

- Active twins often are "harder" on toys. Poorly constructed toys rarely last long. Toys with numerous pieces are impossible to keep together.
- Toys that encourage gross motor development usually are the favorites of racers and joggers. *Durable* indoor and outdoor gym equipment is a good investment.

   Twins of all activity levels are fascinated by:

   1. a large cardboard box,
   2. supervised water play—indoors or out,
   3. blocks —rubber ones are safer,
   4. push-pull toys, and
   5. sturdy, one-piece bead and block loops.

- You still are their most irreplaceable toy. 1. Get down on the floor and become a human jungle gym. 2. Read to twins daily—let each choose the stories.

Can you top this?

   No one has more or better stories to share than a parent of active toddler twins. You may find yourself becoming extremely popular wherever parents gather. You might even consider writing a comedy act and going on tour—after your twins have gone on to the calmer preschool stage, of course!

40

~~~~~~

DISCIPLINE

When you discipline twins, you are guiding them toward acceptable behavior. Twins' interactions lead to unique situations requiring your guidance. Unlike one toddler, a twin may be more interested in pleasing the other twin than in pleasing you. After all, the twin always has more exciting ideas about "fun" behavior than parents.

No!

Toddler twins may hear the word "No" up to four times more often than single toddlers. Twins hear the "no" meant for the individual twin, the ones for the other twin, the ones for the mischief they get into together, and the ones for the extra schemes that only twins can devise. You can eliminate many "nos."

- Have realistic expectations not only for your twins' age and stage but also for their behavioral styles. Each twin is different from the other, and together they are different than having a single toddler.
- Thorough twinproofing eliminates many "nos." (See Keys 37 and 39.)
- Sensitivity to and the anticipation of your twins' individual sleep and hunger needs decreases negative behaviors associated with being overtired and hungry.
- Unless you wish to encourage mischievous behavior, do not describe naughty escapades if there is even a remote chance that one might overhear.
- Give both twins lots of hugs and kisses, plus reinforce positive behaviors, such as sharing and cooperating to decrease either's need to gain your attention through negative behav-

ior. A more difficult to manage twin needs lots of positive reinforcement.

Fighting

Fighting between twins is a common problem. Toddlers do not fight fair. They are too young to comprehend that hitting, pushing, or pulling on their twin can result in injury. It is not unusual for one or both twins to bite the other when frustrated.

Do not interfere immediately in twins' fights unless one is in imminent danger. Observe from a distance. Does the "victim" ever instigate fights? Can he deal with the aggressive twin—even if that means giving up a toy or getting out of the way? If you always "rescue" a victim, your twins cannot learn how to settle conflicts with one another.

Avoiding "rescue" action does not mean you should condone inappropriate methods for handling conflict.

1. Isolating the "aggressor" away from the "victim" for a *few* minutes is the *most effective punishment* for most twins.
2. *Physical punishment* is the *least effective* method. It is illogical to say, "Do not hit or bite your twin," and then punish by spanking or biting the aggressor.
3. Label inappropriate behaviors, and suggest alternate behaviors in very *simple* terms. (You will repeat this strategy many times as they grow!)
4. When a toy is the focus of a fight, the toy's owner could decide whether the other may play with it. (This usually provides an opportunity for a *simple* discussion of sharing.) Give jointly owned toys "time out" on a shelf for a few minutes when twins will not take turns with it. Repeat this when fights recur, or shelve the toy for the rest of that day.

Strategies that work

Ideas that work well with one toddler, such as diverting attention or substituting one toy with another, may be completely undermined by twins' interactions. You may be unsure sometimes whether one or both was involved in mischief, and when you ask, each points to the other and says, "She did it." And toddler twins quickly learn to split up and run in two different directions because they know you cannot run after both at once.

Do not punish both twins unless you *observe* both misbehaving. Collective punishment is not fair to the "innocent bystander" twin. Again, label inappropriate behavior and suggest alternatives. Track each down, however, if you do observe both misbehaving.

"Time out" in a nearby chair is ineffective when the "free" twin entertains the "captive" twin. Try facing a "time out" chair to the wall, or isolate the twin requiring punishment in his room. Five minutes is long enough for toddler "time outs."

Letting each twin make choices cuts down on inappropriate behaviors and defuses many volatile situations, but only suggest choices that are agreeable to you!

- Limit choices to two items. "Do you want to wear a dress or blue jeans today?" "Would you like cereal or eggs for breakfast?" Do not give in to changes of mind, which often occur when twins choose different things. Both need to learn to live with their choices.
- Sometimes a twin's wishes conflict with what must be done. Then the choice focuses on "how" rather than "what" is to be done. "Do you want to get into your car seat, or do you want me to put you there?" "Can you share the blocks, or shall I put them on the 'time out' shelf?"

139

• When either resists your choices, repeat the choices once and tell the twin you will make the choice if she does not. Refusing to choose is in itself a choice. Be sure you follow through with your choice.

Threatening either or both with an unrealistic punishment that cannot be carried out will not improve twins' behavior. Unrealistic punishments are not fair, and not following through with a punishment encourages them to break rules.

The importance of parents

Active and bright twins sometimes wear their parents down until parents "give up" and let them get away with inappropriate behavior. Twins have a right to consistent discipline. They need your guidance. Teaching twins to learn self-control requires a major investment of time and effort, but you will probably continue to use the discipline strategies you are developing now.

41

~~~~~~

TOILET LEARNING

W ho does not look forward to the end of doubled diaper duty? The lure of doing away with twice as many
diapers *is* very tempting, but trying to speed toilet
training only results in frustration for you and for your twins.
Teaching twins to use the toilet is an easy process *when* they
are ready and interested.

Ready or not?

No child can consistently control the muscles used for
bowel or bladder function before 18 months, and this may
occur as late as three years. Mental readiness or interest does
not always coincide with physical readiness to use the toilet.
Although neither twin may tell you in so many words, each
will let you know when to begin. You cannot go wrong if you
let your twins be your guides.

Girls tend to be ready for using the toilet earlier than
boys. This is especially significant for those with boy-girl
twins.

Identical twins often signal readiness at about the same
time. Same-sex fraternal twins may be on similar or very different timetables.

Teaching twins

There are advantages and disadvantages to toilet training twins separately or together. Teaching them separately is
often less confusing, but the process will seem prolonged.
Teaching both means you will have twice the inevitable accidents to deal with at once, but the process will be completed

in a shorter period of time. Of course, you may not have the option of making this decision. Often they make it for you.

- When one is ready before the other, some parents wait until both are ready before teaching either. Move ahead, though, if one lets you know she really wants to try *now*.
- More competitive twins often inspire one another. The last to learn does not like the other twin using the toilet when she cannot.
- Sitting on potty chairs can become "party time" for twins. Leave potty chairs in the bathroom, so they associate that room with going to the toilet. Never make either twin sit on the potty chair for more than 10 minutes. If ready and interested, most use it soon after sitting down.
- Offering an incentive encourages some twins to progress, but keep this low-key so an unready twin does not feel bad. An incentive combined with some twins' natural competition can prove to be truly motivational!
- If either or both do not seem to be getting the idea or continue to have numerous accidents after a week, ask that twin if he would like to wear diapers a while longer. Relax, and try again in a few weeks or months.

Helps and hindrances

There are positive steps you can take to make your life easier during the process of teaching twins to use the toilet.

- You may have cut down on the number of daily diaper changes, but superabsorbent disposable diapers often work too well. Your twins may not know, much less care that they are wet. Switch to less absorbent diapers for daytime use.
- Save the fancy underwear until after your twins have toilet trained. Training pants absorb accidents better. Knowing that "big kid" underwear is waiting can be an incentive for some twins.

- A diaper service can supply training pants.
- Those adorable overalls and pants with zippers, snaps, or buttons are a hindrance when twins must use the toilet *now*. Dresses or T-shirts worn with training pants alone are best during the actual training process. Pants with elastic waistbands are easier for you and your twins to manipulate afterward.
- It is easier to let twins run around in training pants alone if you initiate toilet training during warmer weather.

Potty chairs

You may wonder if you will need one or two toddler potty chairs. The answer to this depends on whether both twins are ready at once and how old they are when toilet learning begins.

- If you think both twins will use the toilet at the same time, then you need two potty chairs. However, you can probably get by with only one. Put one on after the other. Later, twins rarely need to use the toilet at exactly the same time.
- The younger twins are, the more likely they are to prefer small, low-to-the-ground potty chairs.
- Often older twins would rather use the "big potty." A one-step stool makes this easier to manage.
- Some twins feel more comfortable using a potty seat that fits over an adult toilet seat. Also, this can solve the two potty chairs dilemma.
- Boys usually want to stand facing the toilet like Daddy as soon as possible. This can lead to silly situations for girl-boy twins.

Your positive attitude makes a difference

Learning to use the toilet is a big step, and if you use a relaxed approach, everyone will profit. Although potty training probably does not take long if twins are ready, it rarely happens in a day.

- Expect accidents and handle them nonchalantly.
- Do not listen to advice that does not meet your twins' needs. You can introduce each twin to the toilet, but you cannot make either use it. This is something they must be ready and willing to do for themselves.
- If one or both are not ready until late toddlerhood, do not make a big deal of it. They will be ready eventually. Look on the bright side. All those parents of "early learner" twins are making frequent rest room stops when out in their cars or at the mall. There are advantages to everything, even prolonged double diapering duty!

42

PRESCHOOL: THREE YEARS TO KINDERGARTEN

Each preschool twin's horizons expand beyond the other twin, the family, and the home. Twins now become part of a larger community. It is time to meet new friends and begin attending school.

Growth and development

Your twins make great strides in their intellectual, or cognitive, abilities. Although their basic activity levels do not change, new energy outlets become available.

- "Let's pretend" becomes your twins' favorite phrase. Be sure to eavesdrop on their imaginary play. Together twins concoct extraspecial scenarios.
- Preschoolers like to do things for themselves. Twins can dress themselves earlier since they are able to help each other.
- "Taking turns" finally has meaning. Separate outings with each twin are real treats. Devise a system to keep track of whose turn it is to avoid unnecessary arguments or hurt feelings.
- Taking turns sinks in *so* well it is applied to many things: who sits next to you, who pushes the elevator button, who chooses the TV show, and so on.

- "Potty" words are a brief hit with most preschoolers, but this phase often lingers for twins. A single preschooler receives no positive feedback, but twins laugh hysterically whenever either says a word.
- The combined energy of some twin sets still results in a "twin" personality. Its form often alters as twins spend more time outside the home. It might make fewer appearances than before, but when it appears it may be intense. You can "feel" energy building between twins as they work themselves into a "twin tizzy." In the midst of a twin tizzy, twins are oblivious to everything but each other.
- Often the girl of opposite-sex twins "mothers" her brother because girls generally are ahead developmentally.

Preschool and kindergarten decisions

You have more concerns than parents of single children. Read Key 43 in conjunction with this section.

Observe and evaluate preschool programs to find one that suits your philosophy and each twin's needs.

To spend time alone with each twin, some parents send them to preschool or kindergarten on separate days, or they send one for the morning session and one in the afternoon. Most parents send twins together and enjoy a few free hours to themselves—finally!

Twins, especially competitive sets, sometimes work better for someone other than a parent, but preschool is not a necessity. You could work with each or form a play group with other parents.

New friends

Although "real" play is nothing new for twins, it is for the children they meet. Twins apply strategies learned for dealing with each other to new friendships. In turn, new friendships affect the twin relationship.

146

- Twins need additional play experiences with other children. Preschool does not offer enough. "Import" children into your home to play if you do not live in a neighborhood setting.
- Children seem to play best when there are even numbers, as they usually break into pairs.
- Some twin sets ignore a new playmate, but frequently one twin is excluded from play. This can be a shock for a twin who always has had a built-in playmate.
- Twins are so tuned to one another that they may be surprised when other children do not respond in the "right" way, which is as their twin would.
- Some new playmates feel overwhelmed facing twins and play only with one. This is especially true if twins dress alike and approach another child as a united front. However, other children are intrigued by twins.
- Most children can distinguish between identical or similar looking twins quickly, even when many adults cannot.

Toys

Buying toys for two children the same age is more complicated than buying toys for one.

Many twins want the same toys. Sometimes each asks for something different, but both get upset when either does not have what the other twin has. If this becomes a predictable pattern, discuss possible feelings ahead of time. Buy each the same thing if it seems appropriate for your situation. This eventually changes.

Twins should not have to share toys, such as bikes or dolls. A few books, puzzles, or plastic building block sets also should be privately owned.

Big items, like a sandbox, play table, small pool, pretend kitchen, gym set, doll house, race track/garage, big block set, and so on can be shared.

Preschool twinproofing

Preschool twins still require supervision as they interact.

- "Tizzy" twins need more supervision. They easily get carried away, which can lead to hazardous situations.
- Preschool twins can mix fantasy and reality in a dangerous way. They might combine play cooking with real cooking appliances. Sticks and other objects suddenly become swords or medical thermometers to use on one another.
- Preschool twins may encourage one another to sample harmful substances or experiment with matches.
- Supervise joint art time or their projects may extend to your walls.
- Keep active twins closer to you by using wrist cuffs with leashes when out with them.

You and your twins

As each adds new friendships and activities outside the home, your relationship with each twin changes. There is more time to spend with one twin alone.

You still are your twins' best developmental toy. Become sensitive to each one's learning style and take advantage of opportunities for promoting individual development.

It is time to let go of dressing twins alike every day. Clothing choices belong to each twin. Even at this age, when drawers are still filled with duplicate items, twins often express their individuality by choosing different styles. Other sets love wearing look-alike clothing.

Initially it is heartbreaking when one twin is rejected by a new friend. How do you respond? Are they to learn that this is a part of life, or do other children have to take both twins or neither? It can be beneficial for each to be alone for awhile, just as it is beneficial for each to play separately with another child. If you take this in stride, your twins are more likely to accept the situation, too. At first, sympathize with the one left behind and enjoy one-on-one time with that twin. Often preference for one twin flip-flops—a child might play with one twin this week and the other next week.

The payoff period

Most parents feel they have entered the payoff period during their twins' preschool years. Although twin-specific situations still arise, the difficult aspects of parenting twins diminish and the pleasurable aspects persist. It is a joy to watch twins begin to soar, separately and together.

43

SCHOOL: TOGETHER OR SEPARATE?

Any school separation decision *must* be based on your knowledge and understanding of each twin. It is not a lifelong decision. The dynamics of your twins and their classroom change from year to year. You must continue to respond to the needs of each twin by taking their relationship, each one's learning style, and the general makeup of the class into account.

Your twins also should have some say about whether they prefer to be separated or in the same classroom. Talk to each one separately. Sometimes one prefers separation and the other wants to stay together. As their parents, the final word is yours.

Preschool or kindergarten

The first day of preschool or kindergarten often marks twins' first separation from their mother. Asking twins to separate from each other, too, may be more than they can handle. Many single children settle in more comfortably with their best friend. In the case of twins, the best friend just happens to be his twin. Arbitrarily separating twins may deny them the security that others in the class have.

Grade school

Both your twins and the circumstances change. Reexamine your placement decision each year. Teachers and administrators may have some input, but the final decision must remain in your hands. Arbitrary school policies are inappropriate. Your twins' different learning styles, their degree of competitiveness, degree of dependence or independence from each other, and the overall makeup of the class should *all* have an impact on your decision.

The decision

Evaluate the following when you are making your decision about placement.

You cannot force independence. Separation is very difficult if your twins are not ready for independence.

Nursery school classes are often grouped according to birthdays. If you separate twins, are you placing one in a class with children either older or younger than she is?

There are degrees of separation within the classroom and within a school.

1. How much time do kindergarten and first-grade classes spend with each other? Many share story time, snack time, and recess so separated twins may still see each other often.
2. If your twins are in the same classroom, they may be placed in different groups and actually spend little time together.
3. Are children from a specific geographic area placed in one classroom? If so, and you choose separation, one twin will be with known peers and the other will be with strangers.
4. Does separating your twins mean that one must go in the morning and the other in the afternoon?

Interview both teachers. If you sense they communicate often and are sensitive to your concerns about separation, then they will work with you to ensure the success of your separation decision.

If you separate twins in kindergarten, also choose who goes to which class. Ask to see the class list shortly before school starts, and look for which friends are in which classes.

Even if both twins want separation, it still is a tremendous adjustment for them. Give each time to work it out.

Dealing with school officials

Some school systems have arbitrary rules concerning the separation of twins. Of those who have a policy, most insist on the separation of twins. Their assumption is that twins develop better as individuals and are more successful in school if separated. No studies support this. Arbitrary policies for separation deny twins' individuality as much as insisting they stay together when they are ready for separate experiences.

If you find yourself at odds with the administration, the following might be helpful:

- Do not discuss separation in front of your twins. This puts you in a win-or-lose situation with the administration. Once this issue is resolved, you want your children to know that you and the school staff are on the same side.
- State your case clearly and unemotionally. Be assertive but not aggressive.
- Ask to see any policy in writing. It is unlikely that an administrator is able to produce any documentation to support a school's policy on separation. Administrators are often surprised to discover that what they thought was school policy is actually just "the way it has always been done."
- If there is a written policy, ask why it was adopted. Often a parent or teacher thought it was a good idea and passed a resolution without anyone giving it much thought. If an

administrator claims the policy is based on research, ask to see study reports; if she claims it is based on "our experience," ask for a documented comparison of twins separated and left together.

- Remind school officials that each year's decision is not a lifelong decision. Ask them to place your twins as you think they should be for a period of time. If it does not work out, then they can be switched later. This works both ways. The school should be willing to change if their decision is not working.

Consequences

If your twins appear to be happy in their school situation, then you have made the right decision. Have confidence in yourself and your own judgment about what is best for your children. You know them better than anyone.

44

THE EARLY ELEMENTARY YEARS

Twins begin to truly explore their relationship during the early elementary school years. People outside the family influence how each twin sees the other. As they are exposed to new ideas and activities, opportunities for individual expression expand.

Growth and development

You might notice a shift in your twins' relationship as each becomes more aware of himself as an individual.

Your twins may begin to express an interest in extracurricular activities. It usually is best to let each choose her own activities. Sometimes they may want to try the same activity and other times each might want to do something different. Their twinship should not be the basis for activity options.

Other children, and even adults, often have stereotypical images and expectations about twins. They may think fraternal twins are not "real" twins because they do not look alike or are different sexes. Identical twins are supposed to look and act alike and want to do all the same things. For the first time, your twins are confronting twin-related situations without you to run interference. They learn to handle these situations, but your suggestions might be helpful.

One or both twins may resent being called by the "wrong" name, although most prefer this to someone yelling, "Hey, twin." Explain to your twins that other people may forget which name goes with which face. It is OK to let others know when one prefers to be addressed by name, although frequent reminders may be necessary.

Your twins are probably ready for a *simple* explanation of how identical and fraternal twins develop from one or two eggs. (See Key 1.) Descriptive drawings help. Expand on your explanation as they grow.

Twins learn to take advantage of their celebrity without your encouragement!

Twins this age seem to really love, hate, *or* both love and hate each other. Same-sex girl sets, especially identical girls, are more likely to emphasize the twin bond than boys. The love-hate relationship seems more in evidence with same-sex boys, or perhaps their ambivalent behaviors tend to be more obvious.

Either or both sometimes may say they wish they were not twins. They may call each other "ugly," which is particularly amusing if they happen to be identical twins! Neither is rejecting their twin relationship, they simply desire to be recognized as individuals.

Competition can increase as twins "look over each other's shoulders" at schoolwork, report cards, or achievements in extracurricular activities. One may be very upset when the other learns something first, whether it is a math concept or how to ride a two-wheeled bicycle.

As with other behaviors, learning styles are influenced by twin type. Fraternal twins are more likely to have different learning styles, especially girl-boy sets. Identical twins usually have more similar styles. Differences *and* similarities can lead to comparisons and competition *or* cooperation in the form of studying and helping one another.

School

Your twins interact in the school environment for several hours a day. Along with reading and math lessons, both learn a great deal about themselves and others.

- Teachers can also have stereotypical attitudes about twins. It is your job to help teachers perceive your twins as individuals. At the beginning of each school year, discuss with them each twin's strengths and weaknesses and differences and similarities.

- Evaluate each twin's learning style separately. Both twins want to do well and please you. Parents whose twins were premature or had difficulties at birth should be somewhat more alert for signs of learning difficulties and disabilities. Also, more males are affected, so parents of boy-girl twins should not compare their twins. Pursue testing when either experiences great difficulty.

- Make separate appointments for each twin's parent-teacher conference, as you need to talk about each twin individually. If twins are in separate classrooms, ask each teacher how "her" twin is doing in that particular classroom, with this teacher, and these children. Avoid mentioning the other twin's name unless you are asking something specific about their relationship.

- If your twins are in the same classroom, first discuss each twin's progress separately. Then you can ask how they relate during the school day. You need to know if either withdraws rather than competes with the twin, or if one always answers for the other. You do not want this to be the focus of your conference, however, so get back on track if you or the teacher digress to "twins" talk.

Friendships

Peer relationships become a priority during the elementary school years.

Children this age often view friendships with members of the opposite sex with disgust. Obviously, this can have a tremendous impact for girl-boy twins. Both may identify more with same-sex peers or a sibling of the same sex. This is a part of the development of their relationship.

Twins often have both shared and separate friendships. It is up to you to let other parents know your thoughts concerning separate or joint invitations for birthday parties or overnight stays. Even though one twin may feel hurt at the time, do you allow them to have these separate experiences, or do you insist that both be invited or neither may go? Generally, the number of separate invitations evens out. (See Key 42.)

You and your twins

Your twins' relationship always belongs to them, and they must develop it for themselves. You can support and encourage both as they explore their differences and similarities, but you cannot do the work for them. Share your values about cooperation and competition. Avoid comparisons by reinforcing each twin's strengths while helping each work on weaker areas. Step back and let each learn to handle any difficulties that arise between themselves, other siblings, and peers. Your twins' world may be expanding, but your position as their most crucial developmental "toy" does not.

45

SPECIAL SITUATIONS

When one twin is physically or mentally impaired

If one twin is born with a congenital condition or abnormality, extra time is needed to form an attachment with this "imperfect" baby while you "grieve" the loss of your perfect fantasy baby. The presence of a "perfect" twin complicates this process. In many instances, the perfect twin is also the more responsive infant, and naturally a relationship develops earlier with the baby who takes a more active role in your interactions.

The presence of an impairment or deforming condition, whether congenital or related to some other factor, does not negate the "imperfect" twin's need for and right to a strong relationship with you. More than anyone, this twin needs to develop a relationship with you that recognizes and fosters his strengths while it accepts and minimizes his weaknesses.

Hospitalization of one twin

Hospitalizing one twin always has an effect on the other twin as well. Both infant twins need you even if only one is hospitalized. You may feel torn between them.

Some hospitalizations are optional even if they are not presented that way, so question the baby's physician carefully. The doctor may prefer to treat your baby as an inpatient but be willing to treat her as an outpatient once your circumstances are understood.

When hospitalization cannot be avoided, sometimes you can arrange to take both twins. It can be a valid alternative to leaving one at home. Each twin may derive comfort from the presence of the other.

If the well twin cannot stay with you, arrange for someone to bring him to "visit." Some children's hospitals have special residences for patients' families. The sick twin usually needs you more than the well twin. If you are breastfeeding, you will probably need the use of a breast pump to maintain your milk supply.

Most hospitals have relaxed their visiting policies, which helps when an older twin requires a hospital stay. If this is not the case at your hospital, the administration may be willing to make an exception and let the well twin visit. Each needs to be reassured that the other is OK. What either imagines about the other's condition is almost always worse than reality. Help each exchange current photographs and let both talk on the phone often, even long distance when visiting is infeasible.

Single parents
Single parents need to establish a support system. Parenting twins with two parents living in the home is often a monumental task. It is an even greater task for a single parent, unless physical and emotional support is available. (See Key 21.)

If the help you need is not readily available, contact a social service agency. You may find there is help available to the single parent of twins that would not be available if you were the single parent of an only child. Being a single parent does not mean you must do everything for yourself.

Dealing with death
There is such excitement and anticipation when you are expecting twins. If your pregnancy ends in the death of your

twins, you experience not only the grief of losing your precious babies but horror at what has become of your dreams. Your loss is so devastating that friends may have difficulty looking you in the eye because they have no idea what to say or how to comfort you.

The grieving process over the death of any infant, especially twins, takes time. It may be impossible to handle your grief by yourself. Many need to seek professional counseling to accept their grief and move on. (See Appendix B.)

When one newborn twin dies

The death of one newborn twin often interferes with forming an emotional tie with the survivor. It is difficult to go through the grief or the detachment and attachment processes simultaneously. You may postpone grief for the twin who died until you form an attachment with the surviving twin. You might have difficulty getting past your grief to attach to the living twin. You also grieve not only for the loss of your baby but for the loss of "the twins."

You may hear from unthinking friends and relatives, "Well, at least you have one healthy baby," as if that is good enough. Although you rejoice in your live twin, do not let anyone diminish the loss of the other. Your grief would not be greater if this were a single child who died. Refer to the Appendix for more reading on this topic.

When an older twin dies

When an older twin dies, you deal with the loss of your child, the loss of your identity as parents of twins, and the devastating effect of the death on the surviving twin. Other siblings will grieve, but the grief of the surviving twin is more intense. You are asked to give emotionally when your inner resources are depleted because of the magnitude of your own loss. (See Appendix B.)

QUESTIONS AND ANSWERS

We just found we are having twins, and we wonder how we can handle two babies. How do other parents do it?

You do not have to "do it all" on your own. It helps to have someone who stays with you full time while you recuperate from childbirth. Also, most parents say that if they had one thing to do over, they would find some kind of household help for the first few months or years after their twins' births. No matter what type of help you have, though, the helper should alleviate you of housekeeping chores so you are free to care for and enjoy your twins.

My obstetrician refers to my twin pregnancy as "high risk." Does this mean that that there probably will be something wrong with my babies?

Absolutely not! Many expectant parents are frightened by this term. It simply means the potential for your developing a pregnancy or birth complication is higher than if you were expecting a single baby. Now that you are expecting twins, your obstetrician monitors your pregnancy more closely to be prepared for any complication should one arise. Do not allow the potential for complications to cloud your enjoyment and excitement in your pregnancy, however, as many twins arrive after uncomplicated pregnancies and deliveries.

161

My mother-in-law says that all twins are born early and there is nothing I can do about it. Is she right?

Although 45% of twins are born before 37 weeks of pregnancy, (the week considered the cutoff for prematurity), the average length for twin pregnancy is 36.2 weeks. Many twins are carried to full term and have weights that are considered good even for single babies. With proper prenatal care and a good pregnancy diet, you increase the chances of carrying your babies to full term.

My friends say I am more likely to have breastfeeding problems. Is this true?

If lactation or breast milk expression is initiated soon after birth and is followed by unrestricted breastfeedings or frequent pumpings (8 to 12 within 24 hours) and with correct positioning of the babies at the breast, a mother of twins is no more likely to experience engorgement, sore nipples, or latching difficulties than a mother who has given birth to one baby. Plugged ducts and breast infections are not necessarily more common with twins, but delaying or missing a feeding, factors that contribute to these problems, can have a greater impact on your double milk supply. "Nursing strikes," when a baby refuses to breastfeed for several days, are slightly more common with twins than with single babies after the third month. This rarely means that the "striking" twin is ready to wean. Call a La Leche League leader or a lactation consultant for help if you experience any problems.

Friends and relatives are telling me that I will not be able to breastfeed my twins because I will not be able to make enough milk. Is that true?

Fortunately, Nature did not forget that women can have more than one baby. Breastfeeding operates on the principle of supply and demand. Each breastfeeding or breast pumping tells your body to maintain or increase milk production. The more babies you are breastfeeding and the more often you breastfeed them, the more milk your body makes. You know you have enough breast milk for twins if each (1) nurses about 8 to 12 times, (2) soaks 6 to 10 diapers, and (3) has three or more bowel movements every day. Also, each twin should gain about four to eight ounces a week, although a little less in any given week is rarely cause for alarm.

I did not see my premature twins until they were 24 hours old. We missed the bonding that all my friends are talking about. Will I ever love my babies or they love me as much as my friends love theirs?

Yes! Bonding, the formation of an enduring attachment between parent and each baby, is an ongoing process. Bonding with your twins actually begins during pregnancy and continues throughout your lives together. You and your babies have had a poor start, but you can overcome this setback. It may take some time and effort on your part, but you can come to know, love, and appreciate each as an individual.

One of my twins came home from the hospital earlier than the other. Even though I was excited about having twins and I love them both, I am ashamed to admit that I feel closer to the twin who came home first. Is this normal?

Many mothers report feeling closer to the twin who comes home first. You had the time and opportunity to get to know that baby alone, but you never have that luxury after the second twin's homecoming. Do not deny your feelings. Concentrate on responding to and finding one-on-one time with the twin you feel less close to. Eventually, you will feel close to him or her as well.

I feel so isolated since I had twins. My friends do not have the same problems and concerns as mine. Is there anything I can do?

Recognize that your situation is different from your friends and that many of your concerns are unique to twin families. Your best source for support may be another mother of twins with whom you share a similar parenting philosophy and can discuss your twin experiences. Ask your pediatrician, your Mothers of Twins Club, or your La Leche League leader for the name of another mother of twins.

How do I respond to people who say that having twins is the same as having two closely spaced children?

These situations are not the same. People making this comment are usually trying to understand your situation and this seems to be their closest analogy. It is not that one situation is easier or one more difficult. They are simply different.

You automatically view and treat children as different individuals when they arrive separately because you get to know your older child before concentrating on the second. Parents of twins must figure out two infants simultaneously.

Even if siblings are separated by only nine months, they are at vastly different stages of growth and development, and these differences influence your parental approach and the siblings' relationship with one another. It would take two or three years before the behavior of close-in-age siblings might be similar to that of some twins. At that point similarities often depend on the siblings' temperaments and behavioral styles. Also, a third "twin" personality rarely presents itself between nontwin siblings.

Is it OK to dress my twins alike?

There is nothing inherently wrong with dressing your twins alike, especially when they are infants. As they become verbal, however, each should be allowed to choose, within reason, what she wants to wear whether the chosen outfit is alike, similar, or completely different from her twin's. The important point is whether you view your twins as individuals or as a unit, not how you dress them.

Do twins do better in school if they are in the same classroom or separate classes?

Whether to separate or keep school-age twins together should be an individual decision, made yearly, based on your knowledge of your twins. Always remember that you know your twins better than anyone else. Sometimes, one or both twins need the security of being together, especially during the early years. Others relish the independence that comes with having their own friends and teacher. Be sensitive to each twin's needs, and you will make the right decision for them regarding school separation issues.

I am considering having another baby. How likely am I to have twins again?

If your twins are fraternal (dizygotic) and there is a history of fraternal twins in the female partner's family, chances are this partner inherited a tendency for double ovulation. Because of this, you are more likely to conceive twins with subsequent pregnancies than you were with the first twin pregnancy.

Other factors, such as increasing maternal age and a history of prior pregnancy, also play a role. Those taking ovulatory induction agents, or fertility drugs to conceive must ask whether they are taking the same or a different medication. The medication and a woman's sensitivity to it influence the conception of multiples.

Since the conception of identical (monozygotic) twins is believed to occur at random, your chances of having a second set of identical twins are about the same as they were when you conceived before.

GLOSSARY

Activity level one trait of temperament. See *behavioral style* and *temperament.*

Amniotic sac the sac surrounding an unborn fetus, composed of two membranes—an inner amnion and outer chorion—lying one on top of another and filled with amniotic fluid. Also referred to as the *bag of waters* or *membranes.*

Attachment the process of forming an enduring relationship. See *bonding.*

Bed rest a treatment sometimes recommended to prevent or postpone preterm labor or birth or *pregnancy-induced hypertension.* It can refer to lying in bed 24 hours per day or resting with one's feet up several times a day. Its effectiveness is controversial.

Behavioral style the combination of inherited temperament traits resulting in each person's unique behavior pattern.

Bonding the process of forming an enduring attachment with each infant twin.

Celebrity syndrome parental stressing of their children's twinship at the expense of each twin's individuality to increase parental celebrity status. Often associated with *unit thinking.*

Cesarean birth a surgical procedure for delivering an infant through abdominal and uterine incisions. Also called cesarean delivery or cesarean section.

Differentiation the process of determining differences and similarities between twins. One aspect of the parent-twin(s) attachment process.

Dizygotic twins twins derived from the separate fertilization of two different ova and two different sperm, resulting in two genetically distinct zygotes. Also called *fraternal twins* or *heterozygotic twins*.

Embryo transfer placement of an IVF zygote in the uterus. See *in vitro fertilization*.

Family bed the meeting of infants' or young children's nighttime needs for feeding and/or cuddling by allowing them to share their parents' bed for all or part of the night.

Fertility drugs see *ovulatory induction agents*.

Fertilization the union of a sperm and ovum in which their combined genetic material results in a new single cell called a zygote.

Fetal monitor a method for monitoring fetal heart rate (FHR) during labor.

Flip-flopping the alternating, or taking turns, of a particular behavior(s) by twins.

Fraternal twins see *dizygotic twins*.

Gamete intrafallopian transfer (GIFT) surgical placement of ovum (or ova) and sperm in a fallopian tube for fertilization.

Gestation a term for the duration of pregnancy, which in humans normally lasts 38 to 42 weeks.

Heterozygotic twins see *dizygotic twins*.

High risk a pregnancy with the potential for developing one or more complications.

Homozygotic twins see *monozygotic twins*.

Identical twins see *monozygotic twins*.

Idioglossia the rare development of a unique, private language understood only by the children involved.

Intrauterine growth retardation (IUGR) a decrease in the weight and length of an unborn fetus, affecting weight more than length, compared with normal weight and length for gestational age.

In vitro fertilization (IVF) fertilization of an ovum in a laboratory rather than within a woman's fallopian tube.

Low birth weight (LBW) a birth weight of less than 5 pounds, 8 ounces.

Monozygotic twins twins derived from the fertilization of a single ovum and sperm, resulting in one zygote that subsequently divides into two zygotes sharing the same genetic material. See also *identical homozygotic twins*.

Newborn intensive care unit (NICU) a nursery that has special equipment and trained staff members to closely monitor premature or sick newborns. Also called a neonatal intensive care nursery or a special care nursery (SCN).

Ovulatory induction agents hormonal treatment facilitating the maturation and ovulation, or release, of ova. Also referred to as *fertility drugs*.

Placenta the organ in contact with the mother's uterine wall through which oxygen and nutrients for the fetus are exchanged for fetal waste products to be eliminated through the maternal physical systems. Also called the *afterbirth*.

Preeclampsia see *pregnancy-induced hypertension*.

Pregnancy-induced hypertension (PIH) a condition typified by the sudden appearance of high blood pressure, protein in the urine, and fluid retention causing body swelling. These symptoms can result in headaches and/or seeing spots, pain above the stomach area, and/or convulsions. Also referred to as *preeclampsia* or *toxemia* of pregnancy.

Prematurity the birth of an infant before 37 weeks of gestation, which is associated with immaturity of the infant's physical systems and low birth weight.

Preterm delivery the birth of an infant before 37 weeks of gestation. Also called *premature delivery*.

Preterm labor the onset of labor before 37 weeks of gestation. Also called *premature labor*.

Sleep training a euphemism for teaching an older baby

(more than six months) or a child sleep-associating behaviors, so the child can fall back to sleep without a parent's help after night waking.

Small for gestational age (SGA) a decrease in the weight/length ratio of an unborn fetus compared with normal parameters for gestational age. Can be related to *intrauterine growth retardation.*

Sonogram see *ultrasound scan.*

Temperament behaviors that define a person's genetically related *behavioral style.* These genetic traits plus environmental influences lead to the formation of personality.

Tocolytics medications used to suppress, slow, or halt preterm labor to delay or postpone delivery.

Toxemia see *pregnancy-induced hypertension.*

Transfusion syndrome a condition that can occur only when monozygotic twins share a placenta. The result of blood vessel-to-vessel connections within their placenta leading to a disproportionate amount of oxygen and nutrients reaching one twin.

Twin personality a third distinct personality, different from either twin, but resulting from their combined energies.

Twinskin the looseness and puckered appearance of the abdominal skin after some twin pregnancies. Improves to varying degrees with time and exercise.

Ultrasound scan an instrument using sound waves to "see" the fetus within the uterus. Also referred to as a *sonogram.*

Unit bonding the formation of an attachment to twins as a single unit rather than to the individuals within a twin set.

Unit thinking the continued consideration of twins as a single entity.

Zygosity refers to twin set's origin as two separate zygotes or one zygote that completely splits during cell division. See *dizygotic twins* and *monozygotic twins.*

APPENDIX A: SUGGESTED READING

Twin-specific

Ainslie, Ricardo. *The Psychology of Twinship*. Omaha, NE: University of Nebraska Press, 1985.

Alexander, Terry P. *Make Room for Twins*. New York, NY: Bantam, 1987.

Bryan, Elizabeth. *Twins in the Family*. London: Constable, 1984.

Clegg, Averil and Woollett, Anne. *Twins: From Conception to Five Years*. Ottawa, Canada: Deneau, 1983.

Collier, Herbert L. *The Psychology of Twins* (rev. ed.). Phoenix, AZ: Books, 1974.

Friedrich, Elizabeth and Rowland, Cherry. *The Parents' Guide to Raising Twins*. New York, NY: St. Martin's Press, 1984.

Gromada, Karen K. *Mothering Multiples: Breastfeeding and Caring for Twins* (rev. ed.). Franklin Park, IL: La Leche League International, 1991.

Hagedorn, Judy W. and Kizziar, Janet W. *Gemini: The Psychology and Phenomena of Twins*. Chicago, IL: The Center for Study of Multiple Birth, 1974.

Keith, Donald, McInnes, Sheryl and Keith, Louis (eds.). *Breastfeeding Twins, Triplets and Quadruplets: 195 Practical Hints for Success*. Chicago, IL: The Center for Study of Multiple Birth, 1982. (Currently out of print.)

Noble, Elizabeth. *Having Twins* (rev. ed.). Boston, MA: Houghton Mifflin, 1991.

Novotny, Pamela P. *The Joy of Twins.* New York, NY: Crown, 1988.

Theroux, Rosemary T. and Tingley, Josephine F. *The Care of Twin Children: A Common-sense Guide for Parents* (rev. ed.). Chicago, IL: The Center for Study of Multiple Birth, 1984.

Growth and development

Brazelton, T. Berry. *Infants and Mothers: Differences in Development* (rev.). New York, NY: Delta, 1983. (Very helpful if twins have different behavioral styles.)

Faber, Adele and Maslish, Elaine. *Siblings Without Rivalry.* New York, NY: Avon, 1979. (Concrete suggestions for dealing with an intense twin sibling relationship.)

Sears, William. *Creative Parenting.* New York, NY: Dodd, Mead, 1983. (Approach based on individuality of an infant, includes common childhood illnesses.)

White, Burton. *The First Three Years of Life* (rev. ed.). New York, NY: Prentice Hall, 1990. (Stage-by-stage explanations; emphasis on parental involvement; concrete suggestions.)

General breastfeeding (See also Twin-specific list)

Huggins, Kathleen. *The Nursing Mother's Companion* (rev. ed). Boston, MA: Harvard Common Press, 1990. (Thorough but easy-to-read format.)

La Leche League International. *The Womanly Art of Breastfeeding* (rev. ed.). Franklin Park, IL: 1991. (Very thorough, well-researched, and easy-to-read.)

Spangler, Amy K., *Amy K. Spangler's Breastfeeding: A Parent's Guide* (rev. ed.). PO Box 71804, Marietta, GA 30007-1804: 1990. (Covers the basics in a concise, easy-to-read format.)

Prematurity

Harrison, Helen. *The Premature Baby Book: A Parent's Guide to Coping and Caring in the First Years.* New

York, NY: St. Martin's Press, 1983. (Very thorough and well researched; covers negative as well as positive potential outcomes.)

Jason, Janine and Van Der Meer, Antonia. *Parenting Your Premature Baby.* New York, NY: Delta, 1989. (Good general information; chapter for parents of twins.)

Sleep

Ferber, Richard. *Solving Your Child's Sleep Problems.* New York, NY: Simon & Schuster, 1985.

Sears, William. *Nighttime Parenting.* Franklin Park, IL: La Leche League International, 1986.

Thevenin, Tine. *The Family Bed: An Age Old Concept in Childrearing* (rev.). Wayne, NJ: Avery, 1987.

Books for Children

Twinship

Aliki, (Bradenberg). *Jack and Jake.* New York, NY: Greenwillow, 1986. (For toddlers and early readers about individualizing identical twins; currently out of print.)

Brennan, Jan. *Born Two-Gether.* Avon, CT: J & L Books, 1984. (For preschool and early readers about different types and aspects of twinship.)

Hagedorn, Judy W. and Kizziar, Janet W. *What Is A Twin?* Chicago, IL: The Center for Study of Multiple Birth, 1983. (For preschool and elementary school age about different types and aspects of twinship; currently out of print.)

For older siblings of twins

Albertsen, June. *Two Are Twins.* Amelia, OH: *Double Talk*, 1986. (For toddlers and early readers.)

Reich, Ali. *The Care Bears and the Terrible Twos.* New York, NY: Random House, 1983. (For preschool and early readers.)

Twin death

Vogel, Ilse-Margaret. *My Twin Sister Erika*. New York, NY: Harper & Row, 1976. (For elementary school age about identical twinship and death of twin.)*

Periodical publications for parents of multiples

Double Talk, PO Box 412, Amelia, OH 45102. Phone (513) 231-TWIN. Quarterly newsletter for parents of multiples.

The Triplet Connection, PO Box 99571, Stockton, CA 95209. Phone (209) 474-0885. Newsletter for parents of triplets or more.

Twins Magazine, PO Box 12045, Overland Park, KS 66212-0045. Phone 1-800-821-5533, (913) 722-1090. Bimonthly magazine for parents of multiples.

See Appendix B: Resources. Some organizations also publish newsletters.

---

*Currently out of print. You might find books that are out of print at a library.

APPENDIX B: RESOURCES

Twin-specific

The Center for Study of Multiple Birth, Suite 464, 333 E. Superior St., Chicago, IL 60611. Phone (312) 266-9093. Twincare books and research information.

Double Talk, PO Box 412, Amelia, OH 45102. Phone (513) 231-TWIN. Newsletter, resource referral, twin-specific books and pamphlets for parents and children, and equipment.

National Organization of Mothers of Twins Clubs, Inc. (NOMOTC), 1204 Princess Jeanne NE, Albuquerque, NM 87112-4640. Phone (505) 275-0955. Club referral, newsletter, and printed information.

Parents of Multiple Births Association of Canada (POMBA), 4981 Hwy. #7 East, Unit 12A, Suite 161, Markham, Ontario, Canada L3R 1N1. Phone (416) 513-7506. Club referral, newsletter, and printed information.

The Triplet Connection, PO Box 99571, Stockton, CA 95209. Phone (209) 474-0885. Resource referral, newsletter, printed information, and gift items for parents of triplets or more.

Twin Services, Inc., PO Box 10066, Berkeley, CA 94709. Phone (415) 644-0861. Twinline, hotline 415-644-0863, newsletter, twin-related books, and handouts.

Breastfeeding support

International Lactation Consultant Association, 201 Brown Avenue, Evanston, IL 60202. Phone (708) 260-8874. Lactation consultant referral.

La Leche League International (LLLI), 9616 Minneapolis Avenue, PO Box 1209, Franklin Park, IL 60131-8209. Phone 1-800-LA-LECHE. Hotline, LLL group referral, breastfeeding, and childcare books and handouts.

Support for parents of premature twins
Parent Care, Inc., 9041 Colgate St., Indianapolis, IN 46268-1210. Phone (317) 872-9913. Support group and premie clothing referral, newsletter, and printed information.

Support in the event of twin death
Center For Loss In Multiple Birth, PO Box 1064, Palmer, AK 99645. Phone (907) 745-2706 or (907) 333-2935. Networking, newsletter, and printed information for parents after the death of one or more multiples during pregnancy and infancy.

Compassionate Friends, Inc., PO Box 1347, Oak Brook, IL 60521. Phone (708) 990-0010. Parent bereavement support group referral, books, and handouts.

Pregnancy and Infant Loss Center, 1415 E. Wayzata Blvd., Suite 22, Wayzata, MN 55391. Phone (612) 473-9372. Support referral and printed information.

Twinless Twins Support Group, c/o 11220 St. Joe Road, Fort Wayne, IN 46835. Phone (219) 627-5414. For surviving twin.

INDEX

DR. BALTER'S STEPPING STONE STORIES

Dr. Lawrence Balter,
Illustrations by Roz Schanzer

Each of the storybooks in this series deals with a particular concern a young child might have about growing up. Each book features the same cast of characters—the kids who live in the fictional town of Crescent Canyon, a group to whom any youngster can relate. The stories are thoroughly entertaining while they help kids to understand their own feelings and the feelings of others. Engaging full-color illustrations fill every page! (Ages 3–7) Each book: Hardcover, $5.95, 40 pp., 8" x 8"

A Funeral for Whiskers:
Understanding Death ISBN: 6153-5

A.J.'s Mom Gets a New Job:
Adjusting to a Separation ISBN: 6151-9

Alfred Goes to the Hospital: Understanding a Medical Emergency ISBN: 6150-0

Linda Saves the Day:
Understanding Fear ISBN: 6117-9

Sue Lee's New Neighborhood:
Adjusting to a New Home ISBN: 6116-0

Sue Lee Starts School:
Adjusting to School ISBN: 6152-7

The Wedding: Adjusting to a Parent's Remarriage ISBN: 6118-7

What's the Matter With A.J.?:
Understanding Jealousy ISBN: 6119-5

ISBN PREFIX: 0-8120

Books may be purchased at your bookstore, or by mail from Barron's. Enclose check or money order for total amount plus sales tax where applicable and 10% for postage and handling (minimum charge $1.75, Canada $2.00). Prices are subject to change without notice.

Barron's Educational Series, Inc.
250 Wireless Boulevard
Hauppauge, NY 11788
Call toll-free: 1-800-645-3476

IN CANADA:
Georgetown Book Warehouse
34 Armstrong Avenue
Georgetown, Ontario L7G 4R9
Call toll-free: 1-800-247-7160